A God Who Rejoices

And Other Sermons

by
Mitch Robison

Charleston, AR:
Cobb Publishing
2019

A God Who Rejoices, and Other Sermons, is copyright © 2019, Mitch Robison. All rights reserved.

No portion of this book may be reproduced in any way without the prior written permission of the author.

These sermons were meant to be preached, and so the author encourages their use from the pulpit, without the desire to be named as the writer. Use them to the glory of God!

Published in the United States of America by:
Cobb Publishing
704 E. Main St.
Charleston, AR 72933
479.747.8372
CobbPublishing@gmail.com
www.CobbPublishing.com

ISBN: 978-1-947622-40-1

Dedication

This book, and the work that I do, is dedicated to the three souls whom I cherish more than any.

To Katy, my wife, I am thankful for your support throughout the years. You encourage me to pursue my mission. You serve as a great wife and mother of our children. You are a great encouragement to the church and add great value to it. I love you!

To my children, Sadie and Eli, who are beautiful in so many ways, this is for you as well. My hope as a father has been to leave something in this world that would help you through life. The material in this book will help to strengthen your faith and ability to give a defense for the truth. It is my prayer that you will live faithfully for the Lord, that you will honor your mother and I, that you will forever love each other, and that you will serve those around you in an effort to shine your light for Christ. I am so proud of you both and I love you more than words can express.

Mitch's Mission Efforts – Where the Proceeds Go

For a decade, Mitch has served Christians and other individuals suffering hardship—from mowing grass and doing home maintenance (free of charge) for Christians and neighbors unable to afford it or physically unable to do it themselves, to spending weeks in disaster areas helping with clean-up, food distribution, and supply delivery.

Over this ten-year period, Mitch has traveled through much of the southeast region, spending weeks sleeping in Bible classrooms, working in extreme weather, and putting himself through rigorous hours of labor, all in an effort to show that the life of a Christian should be that of a servant. Mitch has traveled to north Georgia following tornadoes, Tennessee following wildfires, Louisiana after floods, and areas of Florida in the aftermath of hurricanes.

Currently, Mitch offers free lawn maintenance and some home maintenance to widows, single parents, disabled, and older members of the church and residents of the community. He volunteers his time and resources to local charities that serve homeless children. He still looks for every opportunity allowed him to work in devastated areas in the region following natural disasters and other accidents. Mitch works with organizations affiliated with the church, such as: "Churches of Christ Disaster Relief Effort" and "Churches of Christ Disaster Response Team." Statements from men associated with these great organizations and others are included below. Mitch also works diligently to serve the family of Christians at the Pleasant Grove Rd. church where he is under the oversight of three shepherds.

The purpose of selling this book is to raise funds for the continuation of Mitch's mission. All monies received, beyond the expense of the production of this book, will be directed to future efforts. There is quite an expense associated with these works, and this is an honest means by which Mitch hopes to raise, through the generosity of his brethren, adequate funds to be able to dedicate more of his time in Christian service. God bless you and thank you for helping this work.

Subject: Work in Baton Rouge Area

My wife Glenda and I traveled to Baton Rouge last week in our motorhome. We stayed on the church parking lot at the Goodwood Church of Christ. That Monday night a young man came to the church building and spent the night in the building and the next day spent all day working with John Pigg cleaning out houses. Glenda and I took meals to various houses that had been destroyed. The next day, I went with John Pigg and his group including this young man and enjoyed getting to meet him and see him work. His name is Mitch Robison and he is the preacher for the Enon Church of Christ in Webb, Alabama. Mitch worked harder than anybody in that group including me. The next day, I went out again with meals and we stopped by the Denham Springs church building and Mitch was there helping that church distribute boxes to those in need. Mitch worked hard and was helpful to everyone that was around him during that week. I want to thank those who helped him make this journey.

Paul Franks
Associate Editor
Magnolia Messenger

"Mitch has been the individual…"

One of the challenges that congregations often encounter when dealing with natural disasters is the lack of individuals to help physically. On multiple occasions, whether tornadoes or hurricanes, Mitch Robison has been there to provide much needed assistance. Mitch has been the individual to help coordinate securing emergency relief supplies and then actively help deliver those items to people in need. God bless Mitch and those working with him to assist congregations of The Lord's Church to reach out physically and spiritually to those in need.

Ken Lowry
Associate Director
Churches of Christ Disaster Relief Effort, Inc.

To Mitch and the Christians you brought with you:

We appreciated the opportunity to have your team join us in our relief work in the Panama City area. You performed excellently and provided a much needed service to our organization and to those affected by the storm. We want to wish you the best in your future efforts and will look forward to having your assistance in the future.

Churches of Christ Disaster Response Team
Mark & Laura Cremeans, Co-Directors

Contents

A God Who Rejoices 1

Back to Jerusalem 5

A Passionate Church 9

How to Praise a Woman 13

Five Great Duties 18

The Importance of Apologetics (Creationism) 23

Describing the Indescribable 27

How to Determine a Biblical Church 31

Daniel: A Test Case in Bible Prophecy (Part One) 35

Daniel: A Test Case in Bible Prophecy (Part Two) 38

A Prayer for the Church 40

All Hands Point Toward Pentecost 44

The Untouchables 48

We Are God's Fellow-Workers 52

False Teachers – Who Are They? 56

Form of Godliness, But No Power 59

Blessed Are The Peacemakers 62

"Are There Few That Be Saved?" 66

What Is Happening to Us 70

Receiving the Blessings of God 74

No One Ever Spoke Like This Man 79

Do Not Be Conformed to this World 84

Dangers in the Church Today (Part One) 87

Dangers in the Church Today (Part Two) 92

Despised and Rejected of Men 97

Can We Really Live For Jesus? 101

Can I Trust My Bible? 105
Does God Really Mean It? 108
Serve God With All Your Heart 113
Christ, Our Passover Lamb 117
Achieving Unity in Religion 121
Between the Sinner and Salvation 124
A Spiritual Workout 128
God – Who Is True 131
Striving For the Faith of the Gospel 134
Sin: From All Sides 138
An Unlikely Place 142
No Man Asked: "What Have I Done?" 146
About the Author 149

A God Who Rejoices

If you were to Google 'an image of God,' you would see numerous images of an old, severe looking man, almost as a task master. I'm not sure where that comes from. First, we have no physical description of God. He is not susceptible to aging so we cannot presume to think He is an old man. Nor can we reasonably think that God is severe. God does hate sin and will deal with it harshly when judgment comes. But the reality of the nature of God is quite different. As the Scripture says, "*God is love*" (1 John 4:8).

The fact is God has reached out to sinners, not to condemn them, but to try to save them.

> *For God so loved the world that He gave His only begotten Son, that whoever believes in Him should not perish but have everlasting life (John 3:16).*

> *But God demonstrates His own love toward us, in that while we were still sinners, Christ died for us (Rom. 5:8).*

God will judge sin, but first He will do all He can to save sinners. And that includes sending His "only begotten Son" to die in our place. Further, there are some things which you and I can do that will actually bring joy, or rejoicing, or delight to God. When we respond to Him in certain ways, God will actually *enjoy* us. We do not serve a God who is gruff, bitter, or miserable. We serve a God who rejoices in His people—when they meet certain standards which He sets. You and I can make our God rejoice when we do the following.

God Rejoices When We Obey

Nothing brings joy to God more quickly than a person who obeys Him.

> *And you will again obey the voice of the Lord and do all His commandments which I command you today. The Lord your God will make you abound in all the work of your hand, in the fruit of your body, in the increase of your livestock, and in the produce of your land for good. For the Lord will again rejoice over you for good as He rejoiced over your fathers, if you obey the voice of the Lord your God, to keep His commandments and His statutes which are written in this Book of the Law, and if you turn to the Lord your God with all your heart and with all your soul (Deut. 30:8-10).*

As Moses wrote these words, He reminded the Israelites of what makes God rejoice. It is simply turning to the Lord with all your heart and soul. It is obeying Him and being careful to observe all of His commandments.

Our world doesn't put much stock in the concept of obedience. Even among Christians, we sometimes stress God's wonderful grace so much that we forget that obedience also matters to Him. In fact, if you want to have confidence that God is delighted in your life, then be careful to observe all of His commands today and every day. If you want to bring joy to the Creator of the universe, then obey Him in all things; do what He says. God rejoices when one of His children is careful to do just as He commands.

King Saul learned this the hard way.

> *So Samuel said: 'Has the Lord as great delight in burnt offerings and sacrifices, as in obeying the voice of the Lord? Behold, to obey is better than sacrifice, and to heed than the fat of rams' (1 Sam. 15:22).*

God did not appreciate Saul's efforts to look religious, or even to follow religious forms, because Saul had been so disobedient. What God wants, and what God enjoys, is that person who will obey in all things. Then the worship and religious forms will be acceptable to God. Do you want God to be happy with you? Learn to obey Him in all things.

God is Pleased When We Are Broken Hearted

> *All have sinned and fall short of the glory of God (Rom. 3:23).*

> *If we say that we have no sin, we deceive ourselves, and the truth is not in us (1 John 1:8).*

The sad reality of life is that each one of us is and/or has been a sinner. None of us has lived well enough to please God. "*There is none righteous, no, not one*" (Rom. 3:10). But, in spite of God's anger at our sin, even sinners can bring delight to God's heart.

We cause God to rejoice when we are convicted of our sin and repent. King David experienced this change after he had committed adultery with Bathsheba, murdered her husband and did other sins in connection with those. But he later wrote,

> *For You do not desire sacrifice, or else I would give it; You do not delight in burnt offering. The sacrifices of God are a broken spirit, a broken and a contrite heart—these, O God, You will not despise (Psalm 51:16-17).*

David knew he could not bring God enough sacrifices to make up for his sin. David knew that even if he brought hundreds of sacrifices, God would not appreciate the act. What David had to offer was a broken heart. The king knew that God delighted in a person who was willing to bring a broken heart to God.

> *For thus says the High and Lofty One who inhabits eternity, whose name is Holy: 'I dwell in the high and holy place, with him who has a contrite and humble spirit, to revive the spirit of the humble, and to revive the heart of the contrite ones' (Isaiah 57:15).*

Our God, who is Holy and who dwells on a high and holy place, actually finds pleasure in dwelling with those who are contrite and lowly of Spirit.

That is why God rejoices and forgives so quickly when we repent. Repentance reflects a broken heart:

> *For godly sorrow produces repentance leading to salvation, not to be regretted (2 Cor. 7:10).*

This kind of change is demanded,

Then Peter said to them, 'Repent, and let every one of you be baptized in the name of Jesus Christ for the remission of sins; and you shall receive the gift of the Holy Spirit'" (Acts 2:38).

When sinners face their sin, feel the emptiness of their broken heart, and turn to God in repentance, He offers them forgiveness of sins and the gift of His Spirit. God eagerly and with joy forgives us and dwells with us, when we offer Him a genuinely broken heart.

The Father Rejoices When We Come Home

In Luke 15, Jesus tells three parables about sinners coming home. The first story tells of a lost sheep. When the shepherd found the sheep,

he lays it on his shoulders, rejoicing. And when he comes home, he calls together his friends and neighbors, saying to them, 'Rejoice with me, for I have found my sheep which was lost!' I say to you that likewise there will be more joy in heaven over one sinner who repents than over ninety-nine just persons who need no repentance (Luke 15:5-7).

Jesus tells us there will be joy in heaven when a sinner is reclaimed by God.

The second story is about a lost coin. When the lady of the house found the coin,

...she calls her friends and neighbors together, saying, 'Rejoice with me, for I have found the piece which I lost!' Likewise, I say to you, there is joy in the presence of the angels of God over one sinner who repents (Luke 15:9-10).

Again, Jesus tells us that there is joy in the presence of the angels of God over a sinner who repents. All of heaven joins in the delight God takes in saving one lost soul. Even if ninety-nine sheep are safe, God rejoices in the one lost sheep that comes home. Even if nine coins are safe and sound, God rejoices in the one lost coin that is found.

Jesus then tells the parable of the lost son. When that prodigal returned home, the father in the story killed the fatted calf and held a great celebration.

'Bring out the best robe and put it on him, and put a ring on his hand and sandals on his feet. And bring the fatted calf here and kill it, and let us eat and be merry; for this my son was dead and is alive again; he was lost and is found.' And they began to be merry (Luke 15:22-24).

The father throws a party to celebrate the return of his lost son. He rejoiced that his son had come home!

All three of these parables describe how God feels when a sinner comes home. It is not a time of dread or somber contemplation. It is a time of delight, a time of rejoicing, a time to celebrate.

What about You?

What is your image of our God? Do you see Him as critical, severe, and harsh? Or do you see Him as loving? Whatever your view of God, know this: If you will turn to Him with a broken heart and determine in your heart to obey Him in all things, you will bring joy to God. You can know that God is rejoicing in your life when you repent, are baptized, and then live for Him. God will be pleased with you. Make God happy today. Turn to Him.

Back to Jerusalem

One of the great pleas of the churches of Christ is to go back and try to restore the New Testament church. That means, all we want to do is follow the Bible, do what it says, and be what it calls us to be. In order to understand what a New Testament church is, I think it is valuable to go back and examine the very first church in the book of Acts, the great church at Jerusalem. If a church, any church, today will follow the example set by the first church, then that church too will be a New Testament church.

> *And they continued steadfastly in the apostles' doctrine, and fellowship, in the breaking of bread, and in prayers (Acts 2:42).*

This verse follows the conclusion of Peter's wonderful sermon. Three thousand people had responded to the message and been immersed in the name of Jesus. These believers must have faced some daunting tasks. How would they all get along, since they came from different parts of the world and had different customs and languages? How would they worship? How would they serve the cause of Christ? The key to their unity, their worship, their service is found in this verse.

They Continued Steadfastly

These first believers who were brought together in the first church had some interesting challenges. They could not go down the street to place membership at another congregation. There was only one church in town, and if they were going to follow Jesus, they had to be part of this church. They couldn't shop for a different church where they would be more comfortable. The solution? They took personal responsibility for the church. "***They continued steadfastly***", that is, they took it upon themselves to make the church work. They didn't lay the job on the apostles. They didn't wait for others to do the work. There doesn't seem to be any of the "them versus us" mentality at this stage of the church's existence.

They took this personal responsibility seriously, as they were ***continually*** (ongoing action) devoting themselves to it. They never took it for granted that the church would succeed. They gave themselves fully to learning the apostle's doctrine, to worship, to fellowship, and to prayer. The thousands of members of this first church accepted the task of making the church succeed, instead of waiting for someone else to do it.

A New Testament church today will be made up of people who do the same. Individuals who do not complain about what "those folks are doing up there at the church", but instead who pitch in and make the teaching sound, the worship meaningful, and the unity a reality. For any church to be like the Jerusalem church, its members need to step up and devote themselves continually to worship, to study, and to fellowship. You will then have taken the church where you worship that much closer to God's will.

The Apostles' Doctrine

The first thing God tells us about this church is of their constant devotion to the teachings of the apostles. The church knew it needed this attention to doctrine for several reasons. First, as yet they had no written revelation about the life and work of Jesus. They had to rely on the inspired words of the apostles. For the church to be what God called it to be, the members had to have a thorough grasp of what the "Good News" really was. Secondly, if they were to spread the gospel message, they had to understand it themselves. And, lastly, if they were to be united they had to come to understand the word of God.

We are not told the details of how these Christians focused on the apostles' teaching. We do see them getting together in many places.

So continuing daily with one accord in the temple, and breaking bread from house to house, they ate their food with gladness and simplicity of heart (Acts 2:46).

It looks as if they assembled as a church to study and learn. And it looks as if they got together in their homes to devote themselves to the word of God.

If you want to be part of a New Testament church you need to devote yourself to learning, understanding and sharing the word of God. Paul would tell the young preacher Timothy in later years,

Till I come, give attention to reading, to exhortation, to doctrine (1 Tim. 4:13).

The reading of the word, the explanation of the word, and the encouragement of the word will move any church toward being a New Testament church. This is important, because too many of us still want to hear what we like to hear, instead of what God said. Paul tells Timothy about that in a later letter.

Preach the word! Be ready in season and out of season. Convince, rebuke, exhort, with all longsuffering and teaching. For the time will come when they will not endure sound doctrine, but according to their own desires, because they have itching ears, they will heap up for themselves teachers; and they will turn their ears away from the truth, and be turned aside to fables (2 Tim. 4:2-4).

Too often we argue about things that are not even in the Bible. We want to hear our favorite topics or issues discussed. But a New Testament church focuses on what God said, just as the very first church did in Jerusalem.

To Fellowship

The first church was devoted to fellowship. This included getting together for worship and in homes. This included sharing their possessions so that no one did without the necessities of life (Acts 2:43-45). But the important part is that they were continually devoted to getting along with one another, loving each other and knowing each other's needs.

One characteristic of a New Testament church is the degree to which its members strive to get along.

Therefore if there is any consolation in Christ, if any comfort of love, if any fellowship of the Spirit, if any affection and mercy, fulfill my joy by being like-minded, having the same love, being of one accord, of one mind. Let nothing be done through selfish ambition or conceit, but in lowliness of mind let each esteem others better than himself. Let each of you look out not only for his own interests, but also for the interests of others. (Phil. 2:1-4).

Paul writes these words to the church in Philippi, which was having some problems getting along. His solution? The members of a New Testament church are to love each other, be united with one purpose, and count the other person (even the one hard to love) better than yourself. To make this church or any other church more like the Jerusalem church, you need to devote yourself to fellowship, to making "the unity of the Spirit in the bond of peace" a living reality (Eph, 4:3). When a church bickers and fights, when members can't stand one another, the New Testament church has not been restored.

The Breaking of Bread

The first church devoted itself to: the Lord's Supper. Although this term can refer to ordinary meals, the meaning here indicates much more than just eating food together. Scholars almost universally agree this particular "breaking of bread" refers to the Lord's Supper.

The early church was united, and one thing that brings unity is an understanding of what the Lord's Supper means. Around the table of the Lord, we see ourselves for what we are, and we understand that all of our brothers and sisters are equally dependent on the Lord's death. The Lord's Supper is a reminder of what Jesus did for us. His body was broken, His blood was shed, all to forgive our sins. At the table we see our sinfulness again; our need for His blood, again; our unity as believers based on His sacrifice, again. The Lord's Supper serves as an equalizer that brings us all to brokenness and dependence on the work of Christ.

For I received from the Lord that which I also delivered to you: that the Lord Jesus on the same night in which He was betrayed took bread; and when He had given thanks, He broke it and said, "Take, eat; this is My body which is broken for you; do this in remembrance of Me." In the same manner He also took the cup after supper, saying, "This cup is the new covenant in My blood. This do, as often as you drink it, in remembrance of Me." For as often as you eat this bread and drink this cup, you proclaim the Lord's death till He comes. (1 Cor. 11:23-26).

Over and over again Paul stresses that eating and drinking are to remind us what Jesus did "for you." He tells us we "proclaim the Lord's death." Jesus' death was for the remission of sins. We proclaim our trust in Jesus' sacrifice for us when we eat. We proclaim that He died for us, all of us. So, in the eating of the Lord's Supper we find our unity. All of us are sinners, all of us are forgiven by His blood. We proclaim this when we eat and drink at the table of the Lord.

In Prayer

Another characteristic of a New Testament church is its devotion to prayer. You cannot watch the Jerusalem church without seeing how much and how often it prayed.

Prayer is a call upon God to act in our lives. Prayer asks God to do what man cannot do.

> *Now to Him who is able to do exceedingly abundantly above all that we ask or think, according to the power that works in us, to Him be glory in the church by Christ Jesus to all generations, forever and ever. Amen (Eph. 3:20-21).*

God is able to do more than we can imagine, and that is according to the power He works within us. God can open doors, God can soften hearts, God can grow churches. We need to call upon God to do these very things.

The early church certainly understood this and devoted themselves to prayer.

> *Praying always with all prayer and supplication in the Spirit, being watchful to this end with all perseverance and supplication for all the saints— and for me, that utterance may be given to me, that I may open my mouth boldly to make known the mystery of the gospel, for which I am an ambassador in chains; that in it I may speak boldly, as I ought to speak (Eph. 6:18-20).*

Paul was in prison as he wrote these words. Yet, he asked the Ephesian believers to pray for the success of His preaching. He knew that God could work effectively, even through a man in chains. So,

> *Pray without ceasing, in everything give thanks; for this is the will of God in Christ Jesus for you (1 Thess. 5:17-18).*

If we are going to restore New Testament Christianity, we must restore the devotion to prayer.

The Lord Added Daily

> *Praising God and having favor with all the people. And the Lord added to the church daily those who were being saved (Acts 2:47).*

Much is being written today about how churches grow. But God gave us the process centuries ago when He showed us the very first church of Jesus Christ. When we make the effort to stand on the word of God in all its truth and challenges, the church will grow. When we make it our aim to be united in fellowship, the church will grow. When we eat the Lord's Supper together, understanding what it represents to us as individuals and to us as a body of believers, the church will grow. When we devote ourselves to prayer, the church will grow.

There are many more qualities of the Jerusalem church that tell us about being a New Testament church. Maybe we will cover some of those in another sermon. But we are told what the very first group of baptized believers did, and we are told by God what the result was. When a church today makes these same efforts, that church will reclaim the place of the New Testament church and God will add people to that church.

If you want to be part of a New Testament church, and if you want to see that church grow, devote yourself to the word, to fellowship, to the breaking of bread, and to prayer.

A Passionate Church

In a previous lesson, we returned to the early days of the New Testament church to examine the very first church, the great church of Christ in Jerusalem. We saw that this New Testament church was characterized by a devotion to the word of God, to fellowship, to eating the Lord's Supper, and to prayer (Acts 2:42). It is still our aim to restore the church today to be like the New Testament church in every way. Part of this requires understanding how the strong churches of the first century functioned, how they worshiped, and how they grew. If a church today will take on the nature of the New Testament church, it can also experience the joy and satisfaction that comes from devotion to the word, to people, and to worship.

To many, the Jerusalem church stands out for reasons beyond its devotion described in Acts 2:42. This church cared deeply about several things, issues they were passionate about. We know they cared deeply because of how they acted. When we go back to the first few chapters of Acts, we see a church that is passionate about some things we need today in order to restore the New Testament church.

Passionate For Worship

And they continued steadfastly in the apostles' doctrine, and fellowship, in the breaking of bread, and in prayers (Acts 2:42).

The first thing that stands out is how much this church cared about worship. They gathered (fellowship) to study (preaching and teaching) and to eat the Lord's Supper and pray (worship). They cared very much about worship toward God and His Son.

So continuing daily with one accord in the temple, and breaking bread from house to house, they ate their food with gladness and simplicity of heart, praising God and having favor with all the people. And the Lord added to the church daily those who were being saved (Acts 2:46-47).

A church today should instill the same passion in its members, a deep hunger to honor God in worship together. This worship was offered in groups of some kind. They met in the temple and in home. But together, they "praised God." Christians today also want to meet together to offer praise to the Almighty God.

Notice an important fact. They were praising God. They didn't merely gather to teach and encourage each other. They didn't merely come together to get their needs met. They came together to offer praise to God. A New Testament church today will also stress the praises of God. In praising God we forget ourselves, we come to know Him better, and we encourage and build each other up, meeting each other's needs. But too often we fail to imitate the early church. They offered praise to God in order to edify and meet needs. That is what New Testament believers should do today.

Passionate For People

> *Now all who believed were together, and had all things in common, and sold their possessions and goods, and divided them among all, as anyone had need (Acts 2:44-45).*

From the very first it is obvious the Jerusalem believers cared intensely for each other. The love was so deep they were unwilling to see anyone suffer or do without. They would even sell possessions, giving up property and income from property, in order to meet the physical needs of the members. This sort of giving does not just come from the obligation to give on the first day of the week. Their giving was generous because they cared for each other.

This was not a passing phase that wore off after they got to know each other better.

> *Now the multitude of those who believed were of one heart and one soul; neither did anyone say that any of the things he possessed was his own, but they had all things in common ... Nor was there anyone among them who lacked; for all who were possessors of lands or houses sold them, and brought the proceeds of the things that were sold, and laid them at the apostles' feet; and they distributed to each as anyone had need (Acts 4:32, 34-35).*

Much time had elapsed from the first converts in Acts 2 to the more mature church in Acts 4. But one thing had not changed: their passion for each other's welfare.

> *"Let no one seek his own, but each one the other's well-being (1 Cor. 10:24).*

God speaks to us today, challenging us to put others first. In place of my wants and needs, I should seek the good of my neighbor. That is what characterized the first church; it should characterize the church today.

> *We then who are strong ought to bear with the scruples (weaknesses) of the weak, and not to please ourselves. Let each of us please his neighbor for his good, leading to edification (Rom. 15:1-2).*

These may seem like challenging commands, but we see the Jerusalem church living with exactly that kind of passion for each other. They put their own needs aside, sold their property and gave it to meet the needs of others.

Passionate For Unity

> *Now the multitude of those who believed were of one heart and one soul (Acts 4:32a).*

One of the great qualities of the early church was its devotion to getting along, to being one. The Jerusalem church took the prayer of Jesus seriously.

> *I do not pray for these alone, but also for those who will believe in Me through their word; that they all may be one, as You, Father, are in Me, and I in You; that*

they also may be one in Us, that the world may believe that You sent Me (John 17:20-21).

The church of the first century understood that how they treated each other had a dramatic impact on the community around them. A unified, loving, caring church would convince the world that the gospel was genuine. A bickering, angry, divided church would only serve the devil's purposes. A church today that wants to restore New Testament practice will have to restore New Testament style unity.

I, therefore, the prisoner of the Lord, beseech you to walk worthy of the calling with which you were called, with all lowliness and gentleness, with longsuffering, bearing with one another in love, endeavoring to keep the unity of the Spirit in the bond of peace (Eph. 4:1-3).

Paul asks us to live as we should, which means getting along with each other so as to maintain unity. One of the reasons God forgave us was so we could learn to love each other. In loving each other we are called on to maintain unity. The reason for our unity is vital.

There is one body and one Spirit, just as you were called in one hope of your calling; one Lord, one faith, one baptism; one God and Father of all, who is above all, and through all, and in you all (Eph. 4:4-6).

Since the message of salvation, the source of salvation, the goal of salvation all stem from a unified purpose, in the same way, the church should reflect just that kind of unity among its members.

Passionate or the Lost

We see the early church caring deeply for more than their own wants or their own people. They cared for the lost around them. So Peter and John go to the temple at the hour of prayer and wind up preaching to the lost (Acts 3). This was not uncommon, but was the standard behavior for believers.

And daily in the temple, and in every house, they did not cease teaching and preaching Jesus as the Christ (Acts 5:42).

The first century church was passionate about reaching out to the lost. In fact, they kept right on teaching in the face of persecution and threats of more persecution.

They went to the temple to preach, not because the temple was important to worship, but because they knew devout Jews would be there. These would be men and women who knew the scriptures and would listen to the scriptures being taught. A church today will go where the people gather, in order to share the message of salvation. This will be done in spite of the obstacles Satan puts in the way. It may be in the work place, in public gatherings in school. Wherever it is, believers should be there sharing the message, because we care about the lost.

They also went house to house. This suggests they found people in private settings in order to study and teach. Whether in public (like the temple) or in private (like homes) they were out sharing the good news of Jesus Christ. A New Testament church today will do the same.

This did not just apply to the 'professionals' who could preach and teach publicly. Again, this seems to have been a passion all the church members shared. When the church suffered a harsh and widespread persecution, the church in Jerusalem was scattered. But, *"those who had been scattered went about preaching the word"* (Acts 8:4). Even in the face of opposition, the early believers cared too much for the lost to keep the message of salvation quiet. They may have to leave their homes and jobs to escape suffering, but they still preached the word.

Passionate About Growth

This church may not have thought too much about growth. They just worshiped with great passion. They just loved each other with acts of selflessness. They just cared intensely for the lost. However, in doing those things they grew more rapidly, more powerfully than most churches today.

In our efforts to restore New Testament Christianity, let each of us renew our concern for worship and make our praise so passionate that we too will be *"praising God, and having favor with all the people"* (Acts 2:47). Let us each love each other so much that each *"esteem others better than himself"* (Phil. 2:3). Let us love the lost with such passion, that we *"cannot but speak the things which we have seen and heard"* (Acts 4:20). Then we will have taken a giant step toward restoring the New Testament church in practice, as well as in preaching.

How to Praise a Woman

Proverbs 31:10-31

A man was walking along a California beach and stumbled across an old lamp. He picked it up, rubbed it—and out popped a genie. The genie said, "Ok. You released me from the lamp .. blah, blah. This is the 4th time this month and I'm getting a little sick of these wishes, so you can forget about 3. You only get one wish."

The man thought about it for a while and said, "I've always wanted to go to Hawaii, but I'm scared to fly and I get very seasick. Could you build me a bridge to Hawaii so I can drive over there to vacation?"

The genie laughed and said, "That's impossible. Think of the logistics of that feat! How would the supports ever reach the bottom of the Pacific Ocean? No, think of another wish."

The man thought about it and said, "I've been married and divorced 4 times. My wives always said that I don't care and that I'm insensitive. So, I wish that I could understand women—to know how they feel and what they're thinking."

The genie said, "You want that bridge with 2 lanes or 4?"

Well, men may not understand women, but one thing we do know is that women like to be praised, and to feel loved. But we also all know that even though men possess this knowledge, they don't use it as often as they should. So today, ladies, I'm going to be your advocate and preach a sermon titled, "How to Praise a Woman."

Guys, would you like to have a wife who's a 10? Well, how about a 12? See, I'm gonna give you 12 things from this text to think about. Now listen, I don't want you to grade your wife. We all know that 10s are unrealistic, and so are 12s. Just remember, you're not exactly perfect either.

And likewise, ladies, I sure don't want you feeling guilty if you don't meet all 12 of these. I doubt that anyone does—for the Proverb gives us the picture of an ideal woman. That's hard to live up to!

The point is that when you find something praiseworthy, you should give praise. Phil 4:8 ends by saying, "if there is any excellence and if anything worthy of praise, let your mind dwell on these things." If you can praise your wife, your mother, anyone for anything, you should.

Likewise, kids, you ought to praise your mom. your grandmother, your aunt, or any woman in the church, for any of these virtuous qualities she possesses.

So here's the list: 12 qualities that are praiseworthy when you find them.

1. (verse 11) "The heart of her husband trusts in her."

I wonder, how many of you praise your wife (or your mom) because you find her to be someone you can trust. In fact, not only can you trust Mom to get something done, but she always has a way of doing it before you ever think about it.

Moms have a 6th sense. How many times have you said, "Honey, can you..." and she just waits for you to finish and says, "I already took care of it"? She does that because she is trustworthy/dependable.

Guys, let me ask you something else that is related to having a wife you can trust. When was the last time you had to worry about your wife making eyes at some other man? You don't do you! Because you can trust in her to remain committed to you. And in doing so, you can also trust that she's not out behind your back talking bad about you or hiding things from you. Trust is vital to a good relationship.

Hey, if the lady in your family is TRUSTWORTHY, you should praise her.

2. (verse 12) "She does him good ... all the days of her life."

That tells me 2 things I want to roll into this 1 point. First, if a wife does you good, that means she builds you up. And let me tell you, we all know that we're not always worthy of all the good comments they bestow upon us. Women have that unique way of telling their husbands and their children exactly what they both need to hear, and want to hear. Indeed, they build us up and do us good.

Moms are the only people in the world who could watch their husband or their kids mess something up terribly and still smile and say, "But you sure looked good anyway."

Second, if a wife does you good all the days of her life, that means she is a close companion to you. Hey, an excellent wife, an excellent mother, is also an excellent companion you love to spend time with.

Good COMPANIONSHIP is worthy of praise.

3. (verse 13) "She works with her hands."

This concept is repeated several times in the proverb. In verses 13, 19, and 24, we catch several images of the mother who sews to meet her family needs. In verses 14-15, we're reminded that Mom does the grocery shopping and then takes time to cook as well. The proverb even reminds us that women often work outside of the home. Verse 16 talks about their "earnings" and verse 24 talks about her "selling merchandise."

When's the last time you thanked your wife or your mother because she sewed a button on your shirt, mended a torn pair of pants, cooked you dinner, or earned some additional income for the family?

Verse 27 says, "She does not eat the bread of idleness." Guys, it reminds us that we're not the only ones working. In fact, I say without any reservation, the ladies have a great influence on the successfulness of the church.

Praise the HARD WORKING woman who goes the extra mile.

4. (verse 15) "She rises also while it is still night." (verse 27) "She looks well to the ways of her household."

That tells me she cares greatly for her family. Oh, how thankful you should be for the wife who gets up in the middle of the night to care for the crying child. And I'm not just talking about newborns. I'm talking about those nights when a child wakes up sick, and you don't even know about it until the next morning. But Mom did. Her ears were tuned in to her child while you were sleeping the night away.

I think verse 15 really alludes to the early morning hours before the sun comes up. Mom's already up, preparing to get the kids ready to send off to school.

I can certainly testify, it's praiseworthy to have a Mom who is always CARING for the family.

5. (verse 16) "She considers a field and buys it." (verse 26) "She opens her mouth in wisdom."

This doesn't just speak to her willingness to work. It speaks to her wisdom. Guys, do you really value the input of your wife? Let me tell you, if you have a wife who speaks with wisdom, you ought to pay more attention. They may just save you from embarrassment a time or two.

On top of that, a wise woman ought to be consulted before you make plans. In fact, I think a wise husband can only be so if he is smart enough to consult his wife before he steams ahead with plans that will only irritate her.

Praise a woman for her WISDOM that she imparts to her family.

6. (verse 20) "She extends her hand to the poor, and she stretches out her hands to the needy."

How blessed you are if Mom is a loving person, not just towards you, but also towards people in the community. Her good deeds become known to all, causing the entire community to speak well of her—and consequently of you, too. It's a blessing to know that people speak highly of her, even when she's not present.

If the woman in your life is COMPASSIONATE, you should feel doubly blessed. What a great quality that blesses everyone.

7. (verse 21) "She is not afraid of the snow for her household, for all her household are clothed with scarlet."

Mom is always prepared. Kids, you ought to thank your Mom every time she remembers something you forget; every time she thinks of something you don't think of; every time she plans ahead and bails you out of a jam. Moms are always so prepared. Just look at some of those purses they carry around!

Praise the woman who is always PREPARED when no one else seems to be.

8. (verse 22) "She makes coverings for herself; her clothing is fine linen and purple."

Guys this is the one you may like the most. Women go to great lengths to look good for you. When she does, you better pay attention and let her know you noticed.

Kids, the same is for you. When Mom dresses up, let her know you think she's lookin' good. Everyone should compliment Mom when she makes herself ATTRACTIVE.

9. (verse 23) "Her husband is known in the gates, when he sits among the elders of the land."

You know what that means? It means she makes you look good! And it may be in spite of the fact that you're a jerk. Hey, if your wife makes you look good—if she gives you a good reputation—you ought to bow down and kiss her feet.

I know several women who continually make their husbands look bad (and that can be for a variety of reasons). Praise be to the wife that makes you look good, who causes you to have an outstanding REPUTATION. Don't take that lightly.

10. (verse 25) "She smiles at the future."

Oh, how pleasant it is to have a Mom in the house who isn't always worried and fretting about everything, but instead is optimistic about what life has ahead of her. Optimistic people are encouragers, dreamers, and help to establish goals. Don't you just love being around optimistic people?

Men, give praise to your wife if she's OPTIMISTIC, looking ahead with pleasure. She just makes your life so much more pleasing.

11. (verse 26) "The teaching of kindness is on her tongue."

Oh, how blessed you are if Mom is a pleasant talker, not a person continually griping and whining about everything. A person who speaks with kindness is a teacher of kindness. Kids, you should thank your Mom if she models kindness in her speech—because it will rub off on you, and you'll learn to speak appropriately.

Men, be thankful if your wife teaches kindness to your kids. She surely makes up for the rough edges you have (and you know what I mean). You know, I can't think of many things that are better than speaking with a woman who always has kindness on her tongue. There's just something special about a kind woman.

A good woman seems to have PLEASANT WORDS for everyone. Why don't you return her love and speak pleasant words to her.

12. (verse 30) "A woman who fears the Lord, she shall be praised."

If your wife, or your Mom, loves God ... you've got it good. Love her, praise her, for her DEDICATION in helping build a Christian home.

CONCLUSION

There's an old proverb that says, "Flowers leave their fragrance on the hand that bestows them." A poem written about it says this:

> *This old Chinese proverb if practiced every day,*
> *Would change the whole world in a wonderful way.*
>
> *Its truth is so simple it's so easy to do,*
> *And it works every time and successfully too.*

For you can't do a kindness without a reward,
Not in silver nor gold but in the joy from the Lord.

You can't light a candle to show others the way,
Without feeling the warmth of that little ray.

And you can't pluck a rose all fragrant with dew,
Without part of its fragrance remaining on you.

Men, women love to receive flowers. That's because they attach meaning to them. Why else would a Mom be so happy to receive a handful of dandelions from her child? She realizes what the flowers symbolize. So men, when we give flowers, we need to remember to attach some meaning to them in our own minds.

But we need to go beyond that and actually verbalize the thoughts and feelings too. Women need to hear our praises—and we need to give them. As the proverb says, the hand that gives the flowers also receives a blessing. We're better husbands and children when we praise our wives and mothers.

So, this Mother's Day, don't just hand your wife a gift—tell her why she deserves the gift!

Five Great Duties

Watch, stand fast in the faith, be brave, be strong. Let all that you do be done with love (1 Cor. 16:13-14).

Corinth was a unique city. It was a port city on a narrow neck of land that connected the mainland of Greece with the Peloponnese Peninsula. It was composed of Roman, Greek, and many other peoples, and as a result, the morality of the city was one of the worst in the entire Roman Empire. But, at the preaching of the gospel by the apostle Paul, many there had become Christians and the Lord added them to His church (Acts 2:47; 18:8; 1 Cor. 1:1-2). But many of their old habits continued to surface in their new lives.

This letter to the Corinthians lists a terrible catalog of sinful conditions. They had been guilty of dividing the believers into mini-denominations (ch. 1-3). Not only was there fornication being practiced by members of the church, but the others simply tolerated it (ch. 5). When brothers in Christ had differences, instead of settling them within the fellowship, they went to law before unbelievers (ch. 6). They had many different problems about marriage relationships (ch. 7). Idolatry and their Christian liberty seemed to conflict (ch. 8). Paul defended his apostleship and right for support of preachers (ch 9). The Lord's Supper had been corrupted and its real purpose ignored (ch. 10-11). There was jealousy over "gifts of the Holy Spirit" and problems over their proper use (ch. 12-14). The climax was their denial of the resurrection (ch. 15). After Paul had addressed the above problems, he then wrote the words on which this lesson is titled, "Five Great Duties."

1. Watch

The Lord constantly warns us to "watch." As we journey through this life toward eternity, we have some company:

Be sober, be vigilant; because your adversary the devil walks about like a roaring lion, seeking whom he may devour. Resist him, steadfast in the faith (1 Pet. 5:8-9).

Just as the devil was deceitful in his tempting of Eve (Gen. 3), so he is with us. We must constantly be on guard, *"lest Satan should take advantage of us; for we are not ignorant of his devices"* (2 Cor. 2:11). We dare not let down our guard, even for a moment.

To "watch" means to be diligent, as Peter wrote,

But also for this very reason, giving all diligence, add to your faith ... Therefore, brethren, be even more diligent to make your call and election sure, for if you do these things you will never stumble (2 Pet. 1:5, 10).

Webster defines this word "diligence" as: "Constant, careful effort." In writing of our entering into heaven, a warning is given:

Therefore, since a promise remains of entering His rest, let us fear lest any of you seem to have come short of it ... Let us therefore be diligent to enter that rest, lest anyone fall after the same example of disobedience (Heb. 4:1, 11).

Constant, careful effort is necessary. No one goes to heaven by accident.

Jesus warned the disciples: "*Watch therefore, for you do not know what hour your Lord is coming*" (Matt. 24:42). In a similar vein, the apostle Paul wrote,

> *For you yourselves know perfectly that the day of the Lord so comes as a thief in the night... Therefore let us not sleep, as others do, but let us watch and be sober (1Thes. 5:2, 6).*

We must heed the admonition to be watchful.

2. Stand Fast in the Faith

Notice that the Bible says, "The faith." To stand fast in the faith, we first must embrace the faith. The apostle Paul declares,

> *There is one body and one Spirit, just as you were called in one hope of your calling; one Lord, one faith, one baptism; one God and Father of all (Eph. 4:4-6).*

Please notice that there is "one faith." There is no choice of faiths, any more than there is a choice of gods! Notice again what God says,

> *Contend earnestly for the faith which was once for all delivered to the saints (Jude 3).*

This faith is not "better felt than told," as some say. It is faith delivered from God:

> *So then faith comes by hearing, and hearing by the word of God (Rom. 10:17).*

But not only must we accept the one faith, we must "stand fast" in that faith. As Paul wrote, in the previous chapter of this letter:

> *Therefore, my beloved brethren, be steadfast, immovable, always abounding in the work of the Lord, knowing that your labor is not in vain in the Lord (1 Cor. 15:58).*

It is characteristic of children to change their minds, often. But we are told,

> *We should no longer be children, tossed to and fro and carried about with every wind of doctrine (Eph. 4:14).*

Instead, let us "stand fast in the faith."

3. Act Like Men (Be Brave, NKJV, But Greek meaning is Act Like Men & Be Brave)

These saints in Corinth had certainly been acting like children in many, many ways. They were "choosing up sides" with regard to which preacher they liked. They were fussing about nearly everything with regard to the worship of God. So, now, they are told, "Act like grownups." Paul wrote them,

> *When I was a child, I spoke as a child, I understood as a child, I thought as a child; but when I became a man, I put away childish things (1 Cor. 13:11).*

This is what we all should do. The same apostle, writing as God directed, said:

We should no longer be children, tossed to and fro and carried about with every wind of doctrine, by the trickery of men, in the cunning craftiness of deceitful plotting, but, speaking the truth in love, may grow up in all things into Him who is the head—Christ" (Eph. 4:14-15).

One thing that will guarantee the failure of a congregation to grow and spiritually prosper is for members to remain in spiritual childhood.

For though by this time you ought to be teachers, you need someone to teach you again the first principles of the oracles of God; and you have come to need milk and not solid food. For everyone who partakes only of milk is unskilled in the word of righteousness, for he is a babe. But solid food belongs to those who are of full age, that is, those who by reason of use have their senses exercised to discern both good and evil (Heb. 5:12-14).

As long as the members in a church bicker and quarrel, that church cannot grow as God wants it to grow. So, in effect, what God is telling them is: "Quit acting like little children. Grow up!"

4. Be Strong

Two things are vital for growth in strength: proper food and exercise. But this strength is not the kind that comes from "lifting weights" to build the physical body. The Lord is speaking of spiritual strength. As Paul wrote,

Exercise yourself toward godliness. For bodily exercise profits a little, but godliness is profitable for all things, having promise of the life that now is and of that which is to come (1 Tim. 4:7-8).

Again he wrote,

You therefore, my son, be strong in the grace that is in Christ Jesus (2 Tim. 2:1).

To develop that kind of strength, we must have the right food:

As newborn babes, desire the pure milk of the word, that you may grow thereby (1 Pet. 2:2).

To "be strong" we must recognize that the source of our strength is not in ourselves.

Be strong in the Lord and in the power of His might (Eph. 6:10).

The apostle Paul, speaking of Satan afflicting him, said:

A thorn in the flesh was given to me, a messenger of Satan to buffet me ... I pleaded with the Lord three times that it might depart from me. And He said to me, "My grace is sufficient for you, for My strength is made perfect in weakness" ... When I am weak, then I am strong (2 Cor. 12:7-10).

When we are doing the will of God, His power is at work through us:

It is God who works in you both to will and to do for His good pleasure (Phil. 2:13).

That principle certainly explains how young David could overcome the Philistine giant, Goliath. He explained how, in tending his father's sheep, a lion and a bear had each stolen a sheep, and he had killed them. He then added,

The Lord, who delivered me from the paw of the lion and from the paw of the bear, He will deliver me from the hand of this Philistine (1 Sam. 17:37).

He wasn't depending on his own skill and strength. He depended on God. This is still what faith is all about. That faith enabled Paul to say,

I can do all things through Christ who strengthens me (Phil. 4:13).

When we are attacked by Satan, may we have the faith that asks (and answers),

What then shall we say to these things? If God is for us, who can be against us? ... Yet in all these things we are more than conquerors through Him who loved us" (Rom. 8:31, 37).

If we are serving God, we are on the winning side!

5. Let All That You Do Be Done With Love

All of the bickering and fussing that these Corinthians had been doing would have ended quickly if this admonition had been obeyed. The great and first commandment is "love God" and the second is "love your neighbor" (Mark 12:30). The apostle had already shown in this letter that it doesn't matter what or how much we do, if it is not motivated by love, *"it profits me nothing"* (1 Cor. 13:1-3). The greatest motivation for any endeavor on earth is love. Jesus said, *"Greater love hath no man than this, that a man lay down his life for his friends"* (John 15:13). Then He demonstrated that love by going to the cross and willingly dying for us.

One of the most compelling verses in the Bible is Heb. 10:24,

And let us consider one another in order to stir up love and good works.

The only way to "stir up love" is to act from a motive of love. We can get people to love us, if we love them. And we can get people to love God, if we demonstrate that love in our own lives. The apostle John wrote,

By this we know that we love the children of God, when we love God and keep His commandments. For this is the love of God, that we keep His commandments. And His commandments are not burdensome (1 John 5:2-3).

When "all we do is done in love," people will look at us in a different way. Jesus knew this, and told the disciples,

A new commandment I give to you, that you love one another; as I have loved you, that you also love one another. By this all will know that you are My disciples, if you have love for one another (John 13:34-35).

With the childish attitude displayed by those saints at Corinth, they could hardly convince the world of the validity of Christianity!

Let us consider deeply the text that we have studied today.

Watch, stand fast in the faith, be brave, be strong. Let all that you do be done with love (1 Cor. 16:13-14).

The Importance of Apologetics (Creationism)

More than 3000 years ago, Moses, armed with divine credentials, walked into the stately presence of Pharaoh, King of Egypt, and demanded: *"Thus says the Lord God of Israel: Let my people go..."*

Amazingly, the monarch replied: *"Who is the Lord, that I should obey His voice to let Israel go? I do not know the Lord..."* (Exodus 5:1, 2). There are numerous souls of this age who proudly boast of being the spiritual descendants of that ancient pagan king. To some, unbelief is a mark of intellectual sophistication in a world that is enamored with philosophy and science. Some boldly proclaim that faith in an Almighty God should be relegated to the realm of superstition—that it makes for nice fairy tales, but is good for little else.

In our day of ever-increasing animosity toward God specifically, and religion in general, it is deemed in some circles as poor judgment at best, and outright foolishness at worst, to proclaim—much less defend—a belief in the God of the Bible. Two questions obviously arise, and these questions I will cover for you this morning: (1) Why is this the case? and (2) What, if anything, can be done about it?

Causes of Unbelief

No doubt there are numerous reasons for the seemingly widespread disbelief in, and antagonism toward, God. Some have a deep-seated disdain for any kind of authority figure. One of the most dangerous contributions a parent can make toward the spiritual delinquency of his child is a failure to instill within him a wholesome respect for authority. If the parent neglects to set the proper example as an authority figure, or refuses to exercise discipline with love, he may be rejected as an authority figure by the child, and thus by transference the child may eventually come to disdain all authority, including the supreme Authority, God. You see disbelief in the goodness of life, skepticism about humanity in general, and the denial of God all sink their roots in the soil of emotion long before exposure to courses in philosophy and science. In fact, I would suggest that the greatest problem is not that our government-funded institutions are teaching things contrary to the word of God, but that our kids today are too weak and ignorant of the truth to be able to stand and defend it!

Another attitude which facilitates disbelief is an unhealthy lust for power wrapped in a cloak of pride. German philosopher Friedrich Nietzsche, who eventually lost his mental faculties, once exclaimed: "If there were gods, how could I endure it to be no god?" Faith in Jehovah simply cannot abide in a heart that is so saturated with inordinate pride.

A third motivation for the rejection of God is the desire to be free of any and all moral restraints. Aldous Huxley, the famed author and atheist, once openly admitted that he rejected belief in God because it interfered with his sexual freedom! These unbelievers reason: If there is a God, I must be morally responsible to Him. I will not be so restrained. Thus, there is no God! The wickedness of man causes him to try to rationalize his situation.

King David pinpointed the problem centuries ago when he asserted,

> *'The fool has said in his heart, "There is no God." They are corrupt, they have done abominable works; There is none who does good (Psalm 14:1).*

Dr. Wilbur M. Smith, in his classic work, *Therefore Stand!,* has noted:

> "One of the reasons why men refuse to accept the Christian Faith is because the very principles of their lives are in every way contradictory to the ethical principles of the Bible, and, determined to remain in the lawlessness of their own sensuality, they could not possibly embrace a holy religion nor walk with a holy God, nor look for salvation to His holy Son, nor have any love for His holy Word" (Smith, 1974, p 170).

Occasionally one may turn to atheism because his faith in someone who professes to be a devotee of God has been shattered. The Proverb is certainly true,

> *"Confidence in an unfaithful man in time of trouble is like a broken tooth, and a foot out of joint (Proverbs 25:19).*

While we may certainly recognize the pain of witnessing the failure of someone in whom we have trusted, we must also recognize that it is sheer folly to blame Deity for the blunders of humanity. Psalm 118:8 reads,

> *It is better to trust in the Lord than to put confidence in man.*

Human suffering has also been used as an excuse by man not to believe in God. The atheist sees undeniable suffering, and assumes that no loving, kind God such as the Bible depicts could ever allow this to occur. All the while the atheist fails to examine the reason(s) behind the suffering, or the purposes which suffering can have. But Scripture provides an answer to the problems of evil, pain, and suffering and in so doing shows us that God's existence is not impugned by such.

Undoubtedly one of the greatest obstacles to a modern-day faith in God is the view that "science" has made such a faith obsolete. Science has become a sacred cow and the laboratory a "holy of holies." While we would not denigrate for a moment the great strides which science has made (and continues to make), and while we gratefully acknowledge all that we owe to science, it is likewise right and proper to admit that science owes everything to God!

But in an era when science has sent men to the moon, eradicated diseases such as smallpox and made extreme advances in diagnosis and treatment of cancer and other diseases, and even unraveled the very mystery of DNA as the "stuff of life," it is easy for man to feel smug and self-sufficient in his scientific knowledge.

Add to that self-sufficiency the ever-increasing popularity of evolutionary thought-which says that there is no God and that man has no master but himself—and it becomes clear that one of the greatest obstacles to belief in God is the pseudoscience of evolution as it is so masterfully foisted upon the minds of men and children in this age.

The Task Before Us

But what can be done about all of this? Is it time to quietly throw up our hands in despair? Must we simply sit idly by and allow the "god of this world" (2 Cor. 4:4) to win the day? Hardly! There is something that each of us can do. Paul, in Philippians 1:16-17 specifically stated that he was "set for the defense of the gospel"- which certainly implies that the gospel can be defended!

And we must defend it, for it is most assuredly under attack. Of primary importance in this battle are these facts:

(1) We are God's people. If we do not proclaim and defend His Word, who will?

(2) God has given us the tools for this defense. Look at 2 Timothy 3:16-17,

> *All Scripture is given by inspiration of God, and is profitable for doctrine, for reproof, for correction, for instruction in righteousness, that the man of God may be complete, thoroughly equipped for every good work.*

This is one of my favorite passages. In this text we read that those tools reside in His word. Let us also look at Romans 1:20-21,

> *For since the creation of the world His invisible attributes are clearly seen, being understood by the things that are made, even His eternal power and Godhead, so that they are without excuse, because, although they knew God, they did not glorify Him as God, nor were thankful, but became futile in their thoughts, and their foolish hearts were darkened.*

Here we see that the tools also reside in His creation. Proper use of these tools, however, is ultimately our responsibility.

(3) If we do not adequately employ the various evidences which provide proof of God's existence as Creator and Sustainer of the universe, men will continue in their unbelief, and as a result will reject His Son and the salvation He came to offer (Romans 6:23).

Suddenly, then, our defense of creation and of Christianity becomes inseparable. One can hardly defend the Gospel system without acknowledging (and defending) God's sovereignty in creation. One cannot effectively proclaim that man fell from a covenant relationship with his Creator, and is therefore desperately in need of salvation from sin, until the fact is first established that there was a Creation and a Fall.

The importance of the Creator/creation concept cannot be overemphasized. In fact, the Lord Himself made that point clear in His discussion in Matthew 19. In the context of responding to the hypocritical Pharisees of His generation, Jesus pointedly asked:

> *Have you not read that he who made them from the beginning made them male and female? (Matt. 19:4).*

Here Christ plainly affirmed that:

(1) There was a beginning;

(2) The first couple was made;

(3) They were male and female.

When Christ spoke of Adam and Eve being "made," He was stressing the fact that this pair was made by acts of creation. As a result, Christ verbally refuted the concept of evolutionary development. And He was certainly in a position to know what took place in the beginning, because John 1:1 tells us that He was there. He was there and Colossians 1:16 tells us that He was the active agent in creation. When men attempt to dismiss Adam as merely a fictional character, they place Jesus in an exceedingly unfavorable light. Adam and Christ stand or fall together, for the Lord said:

> *If you believed Moses, you would believe me; for he wrote of me. But if you believe not his writings, how shall you believe my words? (John 5:46-47).*

Additionally, inspired writers of the New Testament made doctrinal arguments which depended upon the historical validity of the Genesis account. Paul acknowledged that woman is of (meaning "out of") man (1 Cor. 11:8, 12). He called Adam and Eve by name in 1 Timothy 2:13. The apostle considered Adam just as historical as Moses in Romans 5:14, and in 2 Corinthians 11:3 clearly stated that *"the serpent deceived Eve by his craftiness"*.

Look again with me at Romans 1:20, Paul wrote,

> *For since the creation of the world His invisible attributes are clearly seen, being understood by the things that are made, even His eternal power and Godhead, so that they are without excuse.*

The point could hardly be any clearer. The power and deity of the Creator have been perceived, observed, and understood since the creation of the world! Someone (human) had been perceiving and understanding the things that were made "since the creation of the world." This flies in the face of everything macro-evolution teaches. The Lord and His inspired writers affirmed that man has been here "since the beginning of the creation."

Evolutionists affirm that man is a "Johnny-come-lately" who has been here only 3-4 million years out of an alleged Earth history of billions of years. A choice must be made: do we accept and defend the Creator and His narrative of what He did, or do we accept and defend the man-made theory of evolution, which has as its ultimate purpose a repudiation of God's existence?

Who could ever even begin to imagine the numbers of people who have either lost their faith in God, or who have been prevented from coming to Him in humble obedience in the first place, because of the seeds of unbelief? Seeds that were planted at a tender young age, watered by the fountains of infidelity, and fertilized by the false theories of a disillusioned generation? Would we have ever believed that in America, where 70 or so years ago the teaching of evolution was forbidden in public schools, that the teaching of creation would be prohibited? Would we have ever believed that we would lose 60-80% of our young people after they leave for college? Would we have ever believed that this so-called "Christian nation" would be murdering by abortion well over a million innocent, unborn children every year; or that it would no longer define, as God did, marriage as being between a man and a woman? Yet all of this, and much more, has come to be.

"All that is required for evil to triumph is for good men to do nothing." Will we "do nothing"? Or will we rise to the challenge? If we are as unashamed of biblical truth as Paul was, and if we believe that it is *"the power of God unto salvation to all them that believe,"* then our defense and proclamation of it must be as fervent, and as effectual, as that presented in the Scriptures. We are to diligently attempt to proclaim, and defend, the Holy Scriptures. We are to be *"set for the defense"* of that soul-saving message. We must join our hands together in this defense! We must start today.

Describing the Indescribable

As we look at the blessings God has given to us under the gospel of Christ, we must exclaim, just as the apostle: *"Thanks be to God for His indescribable gift"* (2 Cor.9:15). There is no question but that God abundantly blessed under the Old Covenant. But those blessings cannot even be compared with the blessings we enjoy under the New Testament. After all, the word "gospel" literally means, "good news" or "glad tidings." And the good news is that we enjoy blessings in Christ that were never offered to any people before.

One talent that many authors have is the ability to describe the scene or setting of the story. Authors, at least the good ones, can describe a scene and put you into the middle of it, so that you not only read about it, you experienced it. But how does one describe "the indescribable"? What does Paul mean when he uses that expression? In the context, he speaks of the uniting of Jew and Gentile in Christ, as exemplified by the liberal gift the Gentiles gave to Jewish Christians. But, in a broader context, he could well be speaking of the entire gospel of Christ. Let us look at five of these examples of "the indescribable."

The Gift of the Son of God

> *For God so loved the world that He gave His only begotten Son, that whoever believes in Him should not perish but have everlasting life (John 3:16).*

It was no accident that Jesus Christ died on the cross. It was planned. God had purposed the death of Jesus *"from the foundation of the world"* (Rev. 13:8). This is shown in the prophecies of the Christ: His birth, His life, His death. The prophet Isaiah wrote, seven hundred years before Jesus was born, many details about the death of Jesus: rejected, bruised, unfairly tried and condemned, died with criminals, buried in rich man's tomb (Isa. 53). We read in Psa. 22, *"My God, my God, why have you forsaken me?"* followed by the fact that the soldiers would *"cast lots"* for His robe, that people would mock Him and His claim to be the Son of God, and *"they pierced my hands and my feet."* These, and hundreds of other such prophecies, show *"the eternal purpose of God, which he purposed in Christ Jesus"* (Eph. 3:11).

Why did Jesus die? Because *"the wages of sin is death"* (Rom. 6:23), and *"All have sinned and fall short of the glory of God"* (Rom. 3:23). So, He took our place and paid our penalty:

> *But we see Jesus, who was made a little lower than the angels, for the suffering of death, crowned with glory and honor, that He, by the grace of God, might taste death for everyone (Heb. 2:9).*

This idea is stated again in 2 Cor. 5:14-15,

> *For the love of Christ compels us, because we judge thus: that if One died for all, then all died; and He died for all, that those who live should live no longer for themselves, but for Him who died for them and rose again.*

We cannot understand why God loved us so much, nor can we understand how Jesus could take on Himself the sins of all of us. The Bible says it, and therefore I believe it. But the gift is still that "indescribable gift."

The Desire of God to Save Sinners

We read it, and depend on it, but it is still indescribable.

> *For this is good and acceptable in the sight of God our Savior, who desires all men to be saved and to come to the knowledge of the truth (1 Tim. 2:3-4).*

But why would God be so determined to save sinful man that He would offer His only begotten Son as a sacrifice for sin? The answer is love (John 3:16), but that love is still impossible to describe. Even so, Peter wrote,

> *The Lord is not willing that any should perish but that all should come to repentance (2 Pet. 3:9).*

For what kind of people did Jesus die? Not for the righteous or the sinless. But,

> *...when we were still without strength, in due time Christ died for the ungodly ... God demonstrates His own love toward us, in that while we were still sinners, Christ died for us (Rom. 5:6-8).*

We would like to think that, in some way, we deserve to be saved. But that just is not true. God looked down on an immoral world which was in constant rebellion to His will, and sent His Son to die for that world! The simple truth is, sin separates man from God, and God wanted us back. That desire to save sinful man, who could never deserve it, is indescribable.

The Joy of Salvation

Put yourself in the shoes of a man by the name of Barabbas (Matt. 27). You are a criminal, a robber and probably a murderer. You are arrested, and soon to face death for your deeds. You know you deserve the death penalty, but fear and dread of what lies beyond death squeezes your heart until you find it difficult to breathe. But then you are brought out of the cell, and see another prisoner. He has a crown of thorns on his head, he has been beaten until his back is raw, and he is struggling to carry the cross on which he will be crucified. Then you are told, "This man has taken your place. He will die, and you will go free!" If you were that Barabbas, how would you describe your joy?

Our salvation in Christ is much greater than that experienced by Barabbas. When the "good news" of Christ was preached, people responded to it in humble obedience, and *"rejoiced greatly with joy unspeakable and full of glory"* (1 Pet. 1:8). On the day of Pentecost (Acts 2), people believed, repented, and were baptized into Christ (Acts 2:36-38). They then *"ate their food with gladness and simplicity of heart, praising God and having favor with all the people"* (v. 46-47). They then had reason to rejoice! The Ethiopian eunuch relied on the promise of the Lord, *"He that believes and is baptized shall be saved"* (Mark 16:16), and then he *"went on his way rejoicing"* (Acts 8:39). The jailor at Philippi, when he heard the gospel, believed and was baptized, and he then *"rejoiced greatly, with all his house, having believed in God"* (Acts 16:34).

The Blessings That Are In Christ

The apostle Paul wrote of the things which he endured for the cause of Christ:

Therefore I endure all things for the sake of the elect, that they also may obtain the salvation which is in Christ Jesus with eternal glory" (2 Tim. 2:10).

Salvation is "in Christ" and nowhere else! That is why Jesus said, *"No one comes to the Father, but by me"* (John 14:6). The apostle emphasized the same truth,

Nor is there salvation in any other, for there is no other name under heaven given among men by which we must be saved (Acts 4:12).

There is no multiple choice offered. There is no other Savior. If one accepts Jesus Christ and obeys the gospel, he has salvation. If one rejects Jesus, he remains lost in his sins.

The inspired apostle summed it all up in this statement:

Blessed be the God and Father of our Lord Jesus Christ, who has blessed us with every spiritual blessing in the heavenly places in Christ (Eph. 1:3).

However many blessings God gives, they are all "in Christ." That means we have life in Christ (1 Cor. 15:22), all promises are centered in Christ (2 Cor. 1:20), we are saved in Christ (2 Tim. 2:10), we are reconciled to God in Christ (Col. 1:20), we are created anew in Christ (Eph. 2:15; 2 Cor. 5:17), and it is only in Christ that we are made "complete" (Col. 2:10).

The apostle Paul wrote to Philemon about his slave, Onesimus, who had befriended Paul. When Paul sent Onesimus back, he said, *"But if he has wronged you or owes anything, put that on my account"* (Phile. 18). That is exactly what Jesus has done for us! When we accept Him by faith, and are baptized into Him, then He says to the Father, "Whatever he has done, put that on my account." That is indescribable!

The Joys of Heaven

Who can really describe what he has never seen, nor has even had adequately described to him? Maybe if we knew how beautiful and perfect heaven is, we would become unhappy with this life. In any case, God has only given us hints about that wonderful place. Paul wrote,

Eye has not seen, nor ear heard, nor have entered into the heart of man the things which God has prepared for those who love Him (1 Cor. 2:9).

But he was speaking of the gospel age, not heaven. And if the gospel age could not be described until it became a reality, much less can we describe heaven.

Places are important to us because of who is there. Home has a special meaning—not because of where it is, but who is there. Who will be in heaven? God will be there (Matt. 6:9), Jesus will be there (John 14:1-3), our loved ones who died in Christ will be there (1 Thes. 4:13-18), all of the saved will be there (1 Pet. 1:3-4). Can you envision sitting down to talk with your mother and father, and with Moses, Paul, and Jesus? And have all eternity to "catch up" on your visiting?

Can you imagine a place where there is no pain, no death, no tears, no sorrow, no sin? Read Rev. 21, with the beautiful imagery of a perfect place of fabulously expensive jewels and gold which clearly represents the value and beauty of heaven. Who would not want to go to that place!?

But John, in the Revelation, doesn't really describe heaven. He gives us only glimpses and hints. Truly, that wonderful "home of the soul" is really an "indescribable gift."

Although these five things are "indescribable," they are no less real than the air we breathe. We have God's word for that, and *"He is faithful that promised"* (Heb. 10:23).

How to Determine a Biblical Church

A woman tried to sell an old painting in a ragged frame at her garage sale. She asked five dollars. No one was interested. One man offered three dollars, but she held out for five and he would not offer more than three. At the end of the sale, she still had her old painting. She decided to clean up the frame and have it appraised. To her great delight, she found that it was a painting by a well-known artist which was worth more than thirty five thousand dollars! She had a treasure in her possession that was hidden by the dust and dirt of the years.

The same principle can be applied to churches. Many churches look like masterpieces, but they are, in fact, cheap counterfeits. Other churches look like beat up relics that have outlived their usefulness, but are, in fact, the real thing. If one is looking for a church, how can they find the genuine masterpiece, the church of the New Testament that God wants us all to be part of? How can you tell the genuine from the fake? The apostle Peter gives us the way.

> *Since you have purified your souls in obeying the truth through the Spirit in sincere love of the brethren, love one another fervently with a pure heart, having been born again, not of corruptible seed but incorruptible, through the word of God which lives and abides forever, because all flesh is as grass, and all the glory of man as the flower of the grass. The grass withers, and its flower falls away, but the word of the Lord endures forever. Now this is the word which by the gospel was preached to you.*
>
> *Therefore, laying aside all malice, all deceit, hypocrisy, envy, and all evil speaking, as newborn babes, desire the pure milk of the word, that you may grow thereby, if indeed you have tasted that the Lord is gracious. Coming to Him as to a living stone, rejected indeed by men, but chosen by God and precious, you also, as living stones, are being built up a spiritual house, a holy priesthood, to offer up spiritual sacrifices acceptable to God through Jesus Christ. Therefore it is also contained in the Scripture, "Behold, I lay in Zion a chief cornerstone, elect, precious, and he who believes on Him will by no means be put to shame."*
>
> *Therefore, to you who believe, He is precious; but to those who are disobedient, "The stone which the builders rejected has become the chief cornerstone" and "A stone of stumbling and a rock of offense." They stumble, being disobedient to the word, to which they also were appointed.*
>
> *But you are a chosen generation, a royal priesthood, a holy nation, His own special people, that you may proclaim the praises of Him who called you out of darkness into His marvelous light; who once were not a people but are now the people of God, who had not obtained mercy but now have obtained mercy. Beloved, I beg you as sojourners and pilgrims, abstain from fleshly lusts which war against the soul, having your conduct honorable among the Gentiles, that when they speak against you as evildoers, they may, by your good works which they observe, glorify God in the day of visitation (1 Pet. 1:22—2:12).*

Peter gives us several things to look for when searching for the genuine thing.

The Word of God

Peter stresses the role of the word. It is the word that will endure (1 Pet. 1:24-25). It is the truth of that word which we obey, and that process purifies our souls (1 Pet. 1:22). It is the word that has lasting power to save, lasting power to change lives. As individuals search for the true church, they will begin by seeking a church that bases its teaching, its practice, its ministry on the only thing that endures (no I'm not talking about our traditions and preferences)—the word of God.

This will be a church that considers the word to be the authority from God.

> *He who rejects Me, and does not receive My words, has that which judges him—the word that I have spoken will judge him in the last day (John 12:48).*

Any church or group that denies the authority of the Bible, the word of God, may look like a masterpiece, but it is a fake. It is the word that Jesus spoke that will judge us. So, to determine if a church is biblical, it must be a church that teaches the Bible in all things.

But a biblical church will also be one that takes that word and makes it a living process.

> *And the Word became flesh and dwelt among us, and we beheld His glory, the glory as of the only begotten of the Father, full of grace and truth (John 1:14).*

Jesus is described as the living word of God. The Word became flesh. That is, Jesus became human and lived the word of God in the world. As one seeks a biblical church, it will be one that makes the word alive in their bodies. It will be a group of believers who seek to take the words off the page of the Bible and live them in all aspects of life. So Peter tells us to long for the word so that we can grow in our salvation (1 Pet. 2:2).

The Cross of Christ

Peter emphasizes Jesus as the cornerstone which the builders rejected, but which was used by God to establish His new kingdom. Jesus must be at the center of any church that is the real thing. When churches start chasing human issues, human creeds, or human traditions, they clutter up the masterpiece that is the church of the Bible. Eventually, no one can see the real thing, because human creeds, written or unwritten, get in the way.

So, as Peter discusses the priesthood of all believers, the chosen race we are called to be, he stresses the work of the Christ. As Paul says,

> *And I, brethren, when I came to you, did not come with excellence of speech or of wisdom declaring to you the testimony of God. For I determined not to know anything among you except Jesus Christ and Him crucified (1 Cor. 2:1-2).*

Paul had power to do miracles, but he preached Christ crucified. Paul was educated, trained, skilled in the Bible, but he didn't preach his wisdom and knowledge—he preached "Jesus Christ and him crucified." A biblical church must be a group of people who lift up the cross of Jesus Christ in all its teaching, worship and practice.

But, a biblical church will also be a people who lift up the cross in their daily lives.

> *I have been crucified with Christ; it is no longer I who live, but Christ lives in me; and the life which I now live in the flesh I live by faith in the Son of God, who loved me and gave Himself for me (Gal. 2:20).*

The apostle Paul says that he died to himself and now allows the living word to operate through him.

A biblical church is also a people who have obeyed Jesus.

> *If anyone desires to come after Me, let him deny himself, and take up his cross, and follow Me. For whoever desires to save his life will lose it, but whoever loses his life for My sake will find it (Matt. 16:24-25).*

Some churches lift up the cross of Christ in their teaching, but not in their practice. A biblical church is a body of believers who not only preach Christ crucified, but live their lives as if they, like the apostle Paul, have died to self.

The Unity of Believers

Peter says repeatedly that we are all one people, joined together by the common work of God through Jesus Christ. We are told to *"love one another fervently"* (1 Pet. 1:22). We are a *"chosen generation, a royal priesthood, a holy nation, His own special people"* because God has called us out of darkness into His light (1 Pet. 2:9-10). God has taken a bunch of sinners, forgiven them through the blood of Jesus, and turned them into a loving and distinct group of people.

It is this type of behavior that sets the genuine church apart from the fake. The genuine body of Christ is known by its love.

> *A new commandment I give to you, that you love one another; as I have loved you, that you also love one another. By this all will know that you are My disciples, if you have love for one another (John 13:34-35).*

More so, it is how we treat each other that convinces the world we are the genuine body of Christ.

> *I do not pray for these alone, but also for those who will believe in Me through their word; that they all may be one, as You, Father, are in Me, and I in You; that they also may be one in Us, that the world may believe that You sent Me (John 17:20-21).*

Jesus says it powerfully and simply. If we love each other and get along with each other, the world will see that we are the body of Christ. When we fail to love and get along with each other, we convince the world we are not the body of Christ.

Are We That Church?

Paul speaks of "the churches of Christ" (Rom. 16:16). The people he refers to are not just another church trying to do good. They are the churches that claim Jesus, follow Him in His word, and love each other fervently. Does this describe us? At first glance, our worship may seem out of date and worthless. But buried within is a treasure worth much more than a piece of art. It is a treasure that will save souls. But we must not hide this treasure. We must not keep this treasure in a way that Christ is not visible in our lives. That is not a biblical church.

Daniel: A Test Case in Bible Prophecy (Part One)

Infidelity does not admit the reality of Bible prophecy. Since prophecy is one of the strongest evidences for the inspiration of the Scriptures, it is no surprise that it should be repudiated by those who have a biased interest in discrediting the Word of God. Tonight we are going to look at a fascinating account of prophecy in the Old Testament that is worthy of serious investigation. Let us briefly survey the series of predictions chronicled in Daniel 8:1-14, and use it as a test case for the validity of biblical prophecy.

The Prophecy

In the third year of the Babylonian king Belshazzar, Daniel, a Hebrew prophet in captivity, received a remarkable vision from God. As he stood by the river Ulai in the province of Elam, he saw a ram with two horns, one of which was higher than the other. The higher came up last, i.e., it was younger. The ram pushed to the west, north, and south, and no one was able to resist him; he magnified himself and did as he pleased.

Suddenly, from the west there came a he-goat with a prominent horn between his eyes. He was moving very rapidly and his conquests seemed universal. The he-goat charged into the two-horned ram and vanquished him; the ram's horns were destroyed. Subsequently, the he-goat grew in power. At the very height of his prominence, the horn between his eyes was broken, and in its place there grew up four other horns.

Out of one of these horns there eventually grew a little horn which became great in power. It cast down rival dignitaries and trampled them. It assaulted the Hebrew religious system, causing sacrifices to cease and the temple to be violated. Inquiry was then made as to how long this persecution would last; the response was: for 2,300 evenings and mornings. Then would the sanctuary be cleansed.

We do not have to speculate as to the meanings of the vision. It is explicitly declared that the two-horned ram represented the kingdoms of the Medes and the Persians. The rough he-goat was the conquering Greek empire, and the prominent horn between his eyes represents the most illustrious Greek ruler (8:20-21). The "little horn" that later arose was a "king of fierce countenance" who would bitterly persecute the Jews. Yet this horn would eventually be broken, though not by human power. Tonight we will see how history reveals the fulfillment of these divine predictions.

The Fulfillment

It is very important to notice the date when this prophecy was given. It was revealed to Daniel in the third year of Belshazzar. According to the Nabonidus Chronicle, a clay cylinder relating certain events in the king's administration, Belshazzar was "entrusted the army and the kingship" in about 556 B.C. When this prophecy was revealed, no one in the ancient world even dreamed that within two decades the mighty Babylonian empire would fall, much less that Persia and Greece would later become world-dominating influences. It was not a matter that was predictable from the natural human vantage point. But let us consider the historical facts that accord with Daniel's vision.

First, the Medo-Persian empire was a dual power. However, even though Media was the older of the two, Persia exerted far more military authority than did the former (cf. 8:3). According to the ancient historians Herodotus and Xenophon, Cyrus, the Persian monarch (along with his son, Cambyses), pushed the conquests westward to the Aegean Sea, northward to Egypt, precisely as the prophet had foretold (cf. 8:4). The Persian Empire eventually extended from Ethiopia to India, controlling 127 provinces (see Esther 1:1).

Second, from the west (in relation to Persia) came the rough he-goat with the prominent horn. The goat was the kingdom of Greece and the horn represented the "first king over Greece" (1 Maccabees 1:1), Alexander the Great. The conquests of the he-goat were so swift that his feet appeared not to touch the ground as he devoured "the whole earth" (8:5). Alexander swept through Asia Minor, Syria, Mesopotamia, and all the way to India in only twelve years. With an army of only 30,000 he defeated Darius the Mede who had 500,000 soldiers. Richard's Topical Encyclopedia says regarding Alexander: "His success was so extraordinary and his power so mighty that to many he must have seemed divinely inspired." His subjugation of the entire known world was the most rapid that humanity had ever witnessed.

Third, the prophet announced that when the he-goat was strong, i.e., at the zenith of his power, the horn would be broken. In its place four horns would arise. What are the historical facts? Alexander's influence did not gradually wane; rather, he died of a fever in Babylon at the age of 33. After Alexander's death, for a while confusion reigned. Within two decades, however, the Greek kingdom was divided into four segments, under military commanders who assumed the title "kings." Cassander controlled Macedonia, Ptolemy was over Egypt, Lysimachus dominated Asia Minor, and Seleucus ruled Syria. These circumstances are recorded by the historians Diodorus and Plutarch; they are indisputable.

Fourth, Daniel revealed that from one of the four horns, there would arise a "little horn," that vicious persecutor who would exercise his power to the east, south, and toward the "glorious land," i.e., Palestine (8:9). He would cause the sacrifices to cease, and the sanctuary would be defiled. Moreover, this enemy would vigorously attempt to destroy "the holy people" (8:11, 24). Again history has amazingly corroborated the biblical narrative. Antiochus Epiphanes was a ruler out of the Seleucid Empire (175-164 B.C.). He invaded Egypt in the south, he proceeded toward Persia in the east, and he ravaged Canaan in between them (cf. 1 Maccabees 1:17ff; 3:31ff). He plundered the Jewish temple and set up a statue of Zeus in the Holy of Holies. He tore down the wall of Jerusalem and confiscated all copies of the Scriptures that he could find. He forbade circumcision, and offered swine as sacrifices. Anyone consenting to the Law of Moses was under the sentence of death. Forty thousand Jews were slain in Jerusalem and numerous others were sold into slavery.

Fifth, Daniel's vision revealed that the desolation wrought by this Jewish persecutor, along with the desecrations of the holy sanctuary, would last for 2,300 evenings and mornings—then, however, the sanctuary would be re-consecrated (8:13). As a result of the bloody era of Antiochus, the Hebrew people were at an all-time low. Finally the men of Israel revolted. In 167 B.C., an aged

Jew named Mattathias Maccabaeus, along with five sons, declared open war against Antiochus. The "Maccabean Rebellion" continued until Jerusalem was purged of paganism and the temple repaired. On December 25, 165 B.C., the temple was formally rededicated. Thereafter an annual eight-day celebration, known as the Feast of Dedication (or better known today as Hannukah), was observed by the Jews (cf. John 10:22ff).

The 2,300 "evenings and mornings" have been interpreted in various ways, but the most sensible explanation is that they refer to literal days (cf. Genesis 1:5). If one begins at December 25, 165 B.C., and calculates backwards for 2,300 days, he arrives at the date of August 5, 171 B.C. Now, while it is true that we do not possess any historical information at this point to locate some definite event on the 5th day of August in 171 B.C. (the history of this period is rather sketchy), we do know, in fact, that in 171 B.C. there commenced a series of aggressions against the Jews on the part of Antiochus that was concluded only by the tyrant's death. From 175 B.C. until 171 B.C., Antiochus had treated the Hebrews in a peaceful and cordial fashion. In that year, however, events occurred (dependable specifics of which I am unable to find) ignited a rebellion that subsequently brought the wrath of Antiochus down upon the Jewish People. The prophetic chronology of the biblical account is, therefore, perfectly consistent with the history as we know it.

Sixth, it was finally announced that this enemy of the Lord's people would "be broken without hand" (8:25). The expression "without hand" suggests that the death of Antiochus would be an act of God (cf. 2:34, 44-45). The record of Antiochus' death is detailed in both Jewish and pagan sources. When the ruler was returning from Persia, he heard of the defeats of his armies in Palestine by the Maccabeans. Hastening toward Canaan, he vowed destruction to all Jews. En-route, however, he was seized with severe internal (some say bowel) pains. He also suffered a violent fall from his chariot, which aggravated his already desperate condition, and he was forced to halt his journey. His body broke out with ulcers, the stench of which was said to be intolerable. He became delirious. Finally rotting away, he died a miserable death. Documentation for this is found in Thomas Newton's Dissertations on the Prophecies (1830, pp 287-288).

In these prophecies of Daniel 8, there are, of course, many additional details with which we have not dealt in this discussion. We have merely surveyed some of the highlights. These, however, are sufficient to establish our case.

DANIEL: A TEST CASE IN BIBLE PROPHECY (PART TWO)

The Critic's Response

It goes without saying, of course, that the critics of the Bible would reject the evidence of Daniel's prophecies. These skeptics begin with the initial assumption that no such thing as divinely inspired "prophecy" exists, therefore, Daniel, in the 6th century B.C., could not have foretold the details that are a part of this book.

Porphyry became one of the most able pagan adversaries of Christianity of his day. His aim was not to disprove the substance of Christianity's teachings but rather the records within which the teachings are communicated. Porphyry especially attacked the prophecy of Daniel because Jews and Christians pointed to the historical fulfillment of its prophecies as a decisive argument. But these prophecies, he maintained, were written not by Daniel but by some Jew who in the time of Antiochus Epiphanes (d. 164 BC) gathered up the traditions of Daniel's life and wrote a history of recent past events but in the future tense, falsely dating them back to Daniel's time. Porphyry, a 3rd century A.D. philosopher, argued that the events depicted in the book of Daniel **so precisely corresponded with the facts of history** up to the time of Antiochus, that they must be history, not prophecy. If it can thus be established that the book of Daniel actually dates significantly before the mid-second century B.C., Porphyry's analysis of the document becomes a powerful argument for its prophetic character. So we must as ourselves, "Is the Daniel account history or prophecy?"

Consider the following facts relative to the prophet Daniel and the book that bears his name.

(1) The internal testimony of the book is that it was authored by the prophet Daniel (7:2ff; 8:1ff; 9:2ff; 12:2,9).

(2) As a person, Daniel is mentioned in the book of Ezekiel (14:14, 20), and those brief descriptions coincide with allusions in the book of Daniel (28:3).

(3) The ancient Jews believed that no books were added to the Old Testament after the time of the Persian ruler Artaxerxes (464-424 B.C.)(Josephus, Against Apion, 1,8). And they always accepted the book of Daniel as a part of the Scriptures. Hence, they did not believe that it was composed in the time of Antiochus. Other books written during the Inter-biblical Period were rejected from the divine canon; why not Daniel?

(4) Material from Daniel is alluded to as history in the Apocrypha (I Maccabees 2:59-60).

(5) Christ referred to the prophecy regarding the destruction of Jerusalem in Daniel 9:27 and declared that it was "spoken through the prophet Daniel" (Matthew 24:15). If the book of Daniel was a fraudulent production, Christ was either ignorant of the matter, or dishonest about the prophecy's authorship; in either case, His claim of being the Son of God would be nullified.

(6) The testimony of Josephus is decidedly against the late date for Daniel. First, he mentions that Daniel's prophecies regarding Alexander the Great were shown to the Greek general as he came toward Jerusalem in the 4th century B.C., and that the illustrious commander was so impressed that he spared the holy city (Antiquities, XI, VIII, 3-5). Further, Josephus states that the Jewish nation suffered many things at the hand of Antiochus Epiphanes, which, he affirms, were

"according to Daniel's vision, and what he wrote *many years before they came to pass*" (Antiquities X, XI, 7, emp. added).

(7) The precision of details (relative to Babylon) within the book argues that the writer was an eyewitness of that ancient culture, and not a citizen of Judea some three-and-a-half centuries later. It is an indisputable fact that the farther an author is removed from the subject of his narration—both in time and in distance—the more indefinite he becomes with respect to classes, sects, customs, etc. The book of Daniel, however, is very definite with reference to matters that pertain to Babylon. For example:

(a) Daniel is very precise in his use of terms which describe Magi castes (cf. 2:4, 27). Archaeological evidence has confirmed the accuracy of this.

(b) The prophet describes the practice of Belshazzar's wives and concubines eating with the men on festive occasions (5:1-4). This was the custom in ancient Babylon and Persia (Herodotus, V, 18), but not in the period of the Greeks.

(c) Daniel refers to the law of the Medes and Persians (note that Medes are listed first, then Persians-5:28; 6:8, 12, 15); in later history, due to Persia's ascendancy, it becomes the Persians and Medes (cf. Esther 1:19).

(d) Daniel locates the city of Shushan in the providence of Elam (8:2), whereas later, due to boundary relocations, Shushan was in the providence of Susiana. This argues for an early age of the book.

The accuracy of Daniel is so impressive that even some infidels have not been able to escape the force of it. In his infamous tirade against the Bible, *The Age of Reason*, Thomas Paine raises the question as to the authorship of the books of Ezekiel and Daniel. He asks: "Are they genuine? That is, were they written by Ezekiel and Daniel? ... I am more inclined to believe that they were than that they were not ... in the manner which the books ascribed to Ezekiel and Daniel are written agrees with the condition these men were in at the time of writing them" (1974, p 150). What a curious turn of events. Porphyry concedes the agreement of the book with actual history; Paine acknowledges that Daniel authored the book! "He takes the wise in their own craftiness."

(8) Some of the Daniel manuscript discoveries from the Dead Sea scrolls reveal, upon the basis of paleographic evidence, that the original document was composed several hundred years prior to the 2nd century B.C. (Elwell, 1988, 1:573).

(9) Finally, there is this telling point. By the time of the Greek writer Herodotus (5th century B.C.), the name "Belshazzar" (5:1, 8:1) had disappeared from the historical records and was not discovered again until the Nabonidus Chronicle was published in 1882. This is very strong evidence that the book of Daniel was written prior to the 5th century B.C.

The prophetical details set forth in Daniel are astounding. If I may paraphrase Newton (in his discussion of the period from Alexander's death to the reign of Antiochus), there is no historical record so complete, none so concise and comprehensive, as that given by Daniel. No single writer has related so many circumstances, in such exact order of time, as Daniel foretold them. He, even in prophecy, is more perfect than any single historical account—Greek, Roman, or Jewish.

The book of Daniel stands as powerful evidence of genuine prophecy. It is thus a convincing demonstration of the divine origin of the Holy Scriptures.

A Prayer for the Church

The state of many churches today creates concern for many believers. Some worry that churches are too open, too progressive. Some others criticize churches for being too traditional, too unwilling to face the realities of an ever changing world. Still others grow tired of the hypocrisy they think they see in Christians and so give up on the whole idea of church altogether.

What is to be our response to these challenges? It is easy to forget what Jesus promised, *"Upon this rock I will build My church; and the gates of Hades shall not prevail against it"* (Matt. 16:18). Jesus assured His disciples and all of us that Satan and his power, that death, would not prevail against the church. It might seem as if Satan will win, but Jesus promises he will not and cannot defeat the church. Satan might have success in individual lives and in certain churches (think of the seven churches of Asia Revelation 2 & 3), but Satan and death cannot prevail against the church as a whole. Jesus promised us that.

What do we do in the meantime? When we see churches that seem to be in danger from this problem or that issue? What is to be our response to a church that is doing some good things, but also has some problems? The apostle Paul gives us insight into this with his prayer for one of his favorite churches, the church in Philippi. Paul had established this church from difficult circumstances (Acts 16). They had repeatedly helped collect and send money to support Paul in his mission work. Yet, this church had some problems. They were not unified; some were bickering and arguing (Phil. 4:1-2). Although they had helped the gospel in many ways, they had also failed to be all God wanted them to be. So, Paul writes to them and begins his letter with a prayer. Paul describes how and what he is praying for this church of both good deeds and bad.

Be Constant in Prayer

Paul starts dealing with church problems by praying. This seems so obvious, but many of us do it last. Over and over again in Paul's letters (Eph. 1, Col. 1) he tells the local church he is praying for it. Paul prayed repeatedly, constantly, and consistently for the churches. He did this even when churches had serious problems. Paul would never shrink from writing and confronting whatever problems a church had, but he always started on his knees in prayer.

> *I thank my God upon every remembrance of you, always in every prayer of mine making request for you all with joy (Phil. 1:3-4).*

I find it most powerful that Paul tells a church with internal problems that he prays constantly for their well-being. Further, it is powerful to notice that Paul doesn't drag their names before God in dreary, worried tones, but in joy. When Paul prayed for a church, he found reason to rejoice.

I believe this should be the first step in dealing with any concerns we may have for a particular church. We should start by praying constantly for the well-being of the church and its members. Often we start making plans, writing letters, or preparing sermons to deliver so that problems will be faced. While all this may need to occur, we should start by praying first, over and over again for the welfare of the church.

When we start by praying, we may be surprised to discover that there is much reason for joy in the work a church is doing, even if that church has problems. No matter what has happened or is happening in a body of believers, often there is much good being done. Paul writes to the Philippians to confront their problems, but he still finds joy in his prayers.

Be Thankful

> *I thank my God upon every remembrance of you, always in every prayer of mine making request for you all with joy, for your fellowship in the gospel from the first day until now (Phil. 1:3-5).*

Paul begins by telling the Philippians that he is constant in prayer for them. His prayers are not dreary, but filled with joy because of the many good things Paul remembers that they have done for the sake of the gospel.

It is powerful and important to notice that Paul begins his letter to this troubled church with a strong mention of his prayers of thanksgiving for what they have already done. Paul knows they need to clean up their act in some important areas, but before he challenges them on what needs to change, he spends time thanking God for them and telling them there is much to be thankful to God for, in spite of any problems the church might be facing.

If you are worried, start praying for them with a list of all the good things that church has done. I have been a part of several churches. Every church has had some problems, but every church has a rich history of good that has been done. Some of that is simple good deeds that receive no fanfare, such as feeding and clothing the poor. Some of that history of good is found in the many baptisms & souls saved. No matter how severe a church's current problems, we can always make a list of the good that has been done in that church in the name of Jesus Christ.

Further, when you pray constantly, joyfully, and thankfully for the good a church has done or is doing, the problems don't seem so big. We are reminded that God and Jesus will prevail, even if the local church problems don't get worked out to our satisfaction. Taking a church to God in prayer, with a list of all the good done by that church, will remind us not to let Satan look so big and our God look so small.

Be Loving

> *Being confident of this very thing, that He who has begun a good work in you will complete it until the day of Jesus Christ; just as it is right for me to think this of you all, because I have you in my heart, inasmuch as both in my chains and in the defense and confirmation of the gospel, you all are partakers with me of grace. For God is my witness, how greatly I long for you all with the affection of Jesus Christ (Phil. 1:6-8).*

The next part of Paul's prayer for a troubled church still doesn't focus on their problems, at least not specifically. Paul turns to his confidence in them. He says God will finish the work He started in them. Paul's confidence grows out of his knowledge of the church in Philippi, but even more it grows out of his love for those believers. He longs for them with the affection of Christ. He knows they love him and he feels deeply his love for them. This love for his brothers and sisters does not make him alarmed, but confident in what God can do among them.

Imagine how these words would hit a group of believers who are bickering and arguing! They hear from Paul that he is confident they will work things out according to God's wishes. They hear that he loves them and is confident in them that they will do the right things. This must have sobered them up and forced them to consider their actions and attitudes in the problems the church was experiencing.

When we are worried about a church, we should pray with confidence that God will work His way in that church. We should let people know how much we love them and appreciate all the good they have done and then tell them we believe they will do the right thing when all is "said and done." Too often we pray with no confidence and little love. We pray thinking all is lost and imagining all the bad things that are sure to come. Paul didn't pray that way and he didn't communicate that way to a church, even a church with troubles.

The most important aspect of this point is that we should be in love with the local church. Too many of us go to church, we watch the church to see if it is what God wants it to be, but we haven't learned to love the church. Admittedly some churches are hard to love, full of harsh people or arrogant leaders. Paul could see the weaknesses in Philippi, but he loved them so much he still believed in them. We should pray, believing in God that He will answer, and believing in His church that it will do what is right.

Be Smart

And this I pray, that your love may abound still more and more in knowledge and all discernment (Phil. 1:9).

Paul doesn't just say how much he loves, or even just how much they should love each other. He adds to love the need to be smart or wise. He tells these believers he is praying that they will be wise and discerning in what God would want them to do. Too often in church problems, people launch out, using methods that are, at best, worldly—and at worst, just plain sinful. Before Paul launches into dealing with the problems in Philippi, he tells them he is asking God to help them be wise and careful in their efforts.

Again, this part of Paul's prayer is critical in facing the challenges of church problems. We should pray for wisdom and let others know we are praying for wisdom—not for just ourselves, but for all involved. Many church problems would resolve themselves according to God's will if God's people would stop, take stock, be loving and careful in their actions and words. When we run rampant with our wants, ignoring God's will, church problems become church splits and Satan wins a battle. When we are careful and discerning before we act, Satan loses.

Be Sincere

That you may approve the things that are excellent, that you may be sincere and without offense till the day of Christ, being filled with the fruits of righteousness which are by Jesus Christ, to the glory and praise of God (Phil. 1:10-11).

Paul wants them to look at their own motives in all their actions toward the church. So he wants them to be smart, but to know what is good and right. In knowing good, and acting accordingly, they will be sincere and blameless. Paul prays that they will start the healing process in Philippi, not by looking at the actions and motives of others, but by looking inward at their own actions and motives. The solution is found in sincerity from the heart. That is why Paul prays as he does, because right actions proceed from a sincere heart.

The kingdom of Christ cannot be built using Satan's methods. There is no "the end justifies the means" when it comes to the welfare of the church. If you cut God's corners to accomplish God's will you still haven't accomplished God's will! So Paul prays that they will look inward at their own hearts and be sincere. Out of this sincerity of faith and love, they will act righteously toward others in the church.

All For God's Praise

Being filled with the fruits of righteousness which are by Jesus Christ, to the glory and praise of God (Phil 1:11).

Paul closes his prayer with a gentle reminder of what church work is all about. It is about the glory and praise of God. Paul prays this way because he knows church problems don't honor God, they dishonor Him. So he reminds the Philippians they are not in the church to have their own wants met, but to bring praise and honor to God. He says he prays for them so that God will end up with the glory.

Again, this should characterize both our prayers for the church and our actions. Everything we do in confronting a church problem should be based on what will bring glory to God. This should be done in constant prayer, joy, love, and confidence. This should be done with the belief that all will want do what is right and will be sincere. Then, and only then, will God receive the glory.

What about us? I believe much good is being done by the family here. It is likely that there are some areas that need to change, to be better, to be more what God wants. As we recognize and face these issues, let us always do what Paul did. We should start by praying constantly in joy with confidence that the Lord will accomplish His will in us. Then, watch and see how God wondrously answers our prayers.

ALL HANDS POINT TOWARD PENTECOST

There has been much controversy in religious circles regarding the kingdom of God and its establishment upon earth. While some contend that this kingdom was set up during the days of the Old Testament prophets, others point to the days of John the Baptist, or the personal ministry of Jesus Christ, there are still others who assert that the kingdom has not yet been established on earth. But there is only one source of authority for this, as well as for all other religious questions. We must turn back to the word of God for our answer.

In the Bible we find many references to the "church of God," the "kingdom of God," the "body of Christ," the "house of God" and the "family of God." Yet all of these many terms are used to denote the same institution.

As an organism, it is a BODY, with Christ as the head: *"He is the head of the body, the church"* (Col. 1:18), and we as members, *"being many, are one body in Christ, and individually members of one another"* (Rom. 12:5).

In its relationship to God and to the world, it is a CHURCH (a "called out" body of people) that is separated from sin and sanctified for the Master's use: *"But you are a chosen generation, a royal priesthood, a holy nation, His own special people, that you may proclaim the praises of Him who called you out of darkness into His marvelous light"* (1 Pet 2:9).

To show an even closer relationship, this church is referred to as a FAMILY of which God is the Father and Jesus rules as a *"Son over his own house"* (Heb. 3:6). In this family, the members are *"children of God"* (Gal. 3:26-27; 1 John 3:1).

But with reference to its government, it is a KINGDOM over which Christ reigns as King, and Christians are the subjects (Matt. 16:18-19; 1 Tim. 6:15). Each of these terms (and others which could be cited) gives some facet of truth concerning the church of the Lord as God wanted it portrayed.

The Pointing Finger of Prophecy

We have only to look back into the days of the prophets to see the finger of inspired men pointing to the time when the kingdom of God would be set up. Time will not allow all these promises of God concerning the kingdom to be discussed, but we can note a few of them.

> *"Behold, the days are coming," says the Lord, "that I will raise to David a Branch of righteousness; a King shall reign and prosper, and execute judgment and righteousness in the earth. In His days Judah will be saved, and Israel will dwell safely; now this is His name by which He will be called: THE LORD OUR RIGHTEOUSNESS" (Jer. 23:5-6).*

No one can deny that this had reference to the King who would reign over the kingdom of God, and the hand is pointing forward to the future.

The prophet Isaiah also pointed to a future date when he wrote,

> *Now it shall come to pass in the latter days, that the mountain of the Lord's house shall be established on the top of the mountains, and shall be exalted above the*

hills; and all nations shall flow to it ... for out of Zion shall go forth the law, and the word of the Lord from Jerusalem (Isa. 2:2-3).

The prophet in the text stated that the Lord's house would be (1) in the latter days, (2) it would be composed of all nations, and (3) it would go forth from Jerusalem.

After God divulged the secret of a king's dream, Daniel declared,

And in the days of these kings the God of heaven will set up a kingdom which shall never be destroyed; and the kingdom shall not be left to other people; it shall break in pieces and consume all these kingdoms, and it shall stand forever (Dan 2:44).

Again, we see the finger of prophecy pointing ahead to some future time, disclosing some of the secrets of a kingdom to be set up by the Lord. Zechariah pointed to the future, and also listed Jerusalem as the beginning place for God's house: *Therefore thus says the Lord: "I am returning to Jerusalem with mercy; My house shall be built in it"* (Zech 1:16).

New Testament Promises Pointing

When we come into that portion of the Scriptures which is commonly called the New Testament, we still find God's prophets pointing to the future. John came preaching that *"the kingdom of heaven is at hand"* (Matt. 3:2). It had not then been set up, but was "near at hand." Then, Jesus began to preach, and His message was the same: *"Repent, for the kingdom of heaven is at hand"* (Matt. 4:17). The kingdom was, at that time, yet in the future. But Jesus promised the apostles, *"There are some standing here who will not taste death till they see the kingdom of God present with power"* (Mark 9:1). So, the kingdom was yet future, but it would come during the lifetime of the apostles.

Notice this promise of the Lord Jesus,

On this rock I will build My church, and the gates of Hades shall not prevail against it. And I will give you the keys of the kingdom of heaven, and whatever you bind on earth will be bound in heaven, and whatever you loose on earth will be loosed in heaven (Matt 16:18-19).

Now, if the church and the kingdom here referred to are not one and the same thing, then Jesus pulled a colossal architectural blunder in turning over to the apostles the wrong set of keys! On a later occasion, Jesus again pointed ahead to the beginning of the church, or kingdom (Luke 22:16-18).

When He gave His disciples a model prayer, Jesus taught them to pray for the coming of the kingdom (Matt. 6:10). It had not been set up at that time, but was yet future. He sent out His disciples with instructions to preach, *"The kingdom of God has come near to you"* (Luke 10:9). During the ministry of Jesus on the earth, he instructed the apostles and other disciples to look for and to pray for the coming of the kingdom. It was yet future.

The Fingers Point Back

With the day of Pentecost, after the death, burial, and resurrection of Jesus, all hands point in a different direction. The finger turned to that which had already happened. Do you recall God's promise in Jer. 23:5? Go back and study that prophecy carefully and compare it with Acts 2:29-31, which was preached on that day of Pentecost. There you will see that Jesus Christ was brought forth from the grave to sit on the throne of David! To reign, He must have a kingdom. It had then been established, with the Lord Jesus as the King. The apostle Peter set forth in that first gospel sermon the "Magna Carta" of heaven's rule, and people were invited to be subjects of the kingdom of Christ.

Later, we find inspired men preaching the things concerning the kingdom of God and of Christ (Acts 8:12; 14:22; 28:23). The apostle Paul defined the kingdom (Rom. 14:17; 1 Cor. 4:20). He taught concerning the duration of the kingdom, showing that it would endure until the return of the Lord Jesus, when He would deliver the kingdom back to the Father (1 Cor. 15:24-25). Paul, in Col. 1:13, declared that God has *"delivered us from the power of darkness and conveyed us into the kingdom of the Son of His love."* So, we *"are receiving a kingdom which cannot be shaken"* (Heb. 12:28). John also wrote that he and all other Christians were in that kingdom (Rev. 1:9). We find that every reference in the writings of the apostles shows that the kingdom had been established. Pentecost had become the pivotal point, because the church was established then.

Prophecy Fulfilled at Pentecost

Let us consider how prophecy was fulfilled on this "great and notable day" of Pentecost. First, Isaiah's prophecy concerning "the last days" was pointedly fulfilled, for Peter said expressly that the events of this day fulfilled the "last days" prophecy (Acts 2:16-17). Also, we find the prophecy of "all nations" fulfilled, since all nations were represented in the audience that day (Acts 2:5). Later, the Gentiles were brought in by this message that began on Pentecost (Acts 10; see also Acts 11:15). Too, the "house of God" had its beginning, as promised, in the city of Jerusalem, thus fulfilling the prophecies of Zech. 1:16; Isa. 2:2-3 and Luke 24:46-49.

It was on this day of Pentecost, as recorded in Acts 2, that the "repentance and remission of sins" (Luke 24:47) was preached for the first time after the resurrection of Jesus. Just before His ascension, Jesus was asked by His disciples if He would now "restore the kingdom to Israel" (Acts 1:6). His reply was,

> *It is not for you to know times or seasons which the Father has put in His own authority. But you shall receive power when the Holy Spirit has come upon you; and you shall be witnesses to Me in Jerusalem, and in all Judea and Samaria, and to the end of the earth (Acts 1:7-8).*

Jesus had said that the *"kingdom shall come with power"* (Mark 9:1). The apostles were told to wait in Jerusalem until they were *"clothed with power from on high"* (Luke 24:49). And now, in the city of Jerusalem, Jesus tells the disciples to wait, *"You shall receive power when the Holy Spirit comes upon you"* (Acts 1:8). The Holy Spirit came on this day of Pentecost (Acts 2:1-4), and at that point all the prophecies come together—fulfilled on this day of Pentecost in the city of Jerusalem.

Before Pentecost, all hands point forward to a time when the prophecies of the kingdom/church would be fulfilled. After Pentecost, all hands point back to that time when the kingdom/church was established. The climax comes as we look more closely at the events of that day. The apostle

Peter preached Jesus to be the Christ, the Son of God. When people asked what to do, they were told:

> *Repent, and let everyone of you be baptized in the name of Jesus Christ for the remission of sins; and you shall receive the gift of the Holy Spirit ... Then those who gladly received his word were baptized; and that day about three thousand souls were added to them ... And the Lord added to the church daily those who were being saved (Acts 2:38, 41, 47).*

That which had been promised by the Lord had now become a reality. What the prophets had foretold—about the kingdom, the church, the house (family) of God—had now been established or built, and those people who had been saved had been added to it.

Isn't it great to know that we are a part of that kingdom? The kingdom is here now, and if you are a Christian, you are part of that kingdom. If you are not a Christian, why wait? Be part of the family of God. Confess Christ as the Son of God. Be baptized for the forgiveness of your sins. Rise to walk in newness of life. A life dedicated to faithful living in the Lord.

The Untouchables

Elliot Ness was an incorruptible special agent in Chicago. He was the renowned untouchable. The label was given to him because he was unwilling to take a bribe as a law enforcement officer. In an era when many law enforcement officials at all levels were taking money from criminals, Ness and his men were untouchable.

Long before there was a crime fighting unit, there was another group of people who were literally untouchable. They could not just enter into a community. Where ever they went they had to cry out in warning to others. They were the lepers of ancient times.

These unfortunate victims were defined as unclean under the Law of Moses. There were strict guidelines to follow to determine if a person was unclean due to the problems of leprosy.

> *Now the leper on whom the sore is, his clothes shall be torn and his head bare; and he shall cover his mustache, and cry, 'Unclean! Unclean!' He shall be unclean. All the days he has the sore he shall be unclean. He is unclean, and he shall dwell alone; his dwelling shall be outside the camp (Lev. 13:45-46).*

If the disease was present, the victim was sent to live outside the camp, away from all other people.

These lepers were literally untouchables, and were to cry "unclean" anywhere they went, so that healthy people would not come in contact with them and come down with the disease. They could not have a normal home life. They could not worship with other believers. Anyone who came in contact with a leper was considered unclean as well. So, they were social, spiritual, and physical outcasts. They were condemned to a life of isolation and ostracism by all of the healthy members of the community.

Mark tells us a powerful story about one such untouchable. Word had already spread about Jesus' power to heal. One leper decided to go have a little talk with Jesus.

> *Now a leper came to Him, imploring Him, kneeling down to Him and saying to Him, "If You are willing, You can make me clean." Then Jesus, moved with compassion, stretched out His hand and touched him, and said to him, "I am willing; be cleansed." As soon as He had spoken, immediately the leprosy left him, and he was cleansed. And He strictly warned him and sent him away at once, and said to him, "See that you say nothing to anyone; but go your way, show yourself to the priest, and offer for your cleansing those things which Moses commanded, as a testimony to them." However, he went out and began to proclaim it freely, and to spread the matter, so that Jesus could no longer openly enter the city, but was outside in deserted places; and they came to Him from every direction (Mark 1:40-45).*

This encounter between Jesus and an untouchable can teach us many lessons.

All Sin Is Ugly

God chose skin diseases such as leprosy to stand as a symbol for sin. God probably had many reasons for doing this. Such diseases are often highly contagious, so the Lord wanted people to be protected from contamination by coming in contact with lepers. But God also wanted people to see how He views sin. He did this by choosing a disease that was ugly in all its forms. God wanted mankind to see how ugly sin looks to Him.

Leprosy was horrible in all its consequences. Physically, the sufferer could lose fingers, toes, ears and more as the disease progressed. If the disease continued, it would lead to death. Moreover, the victim could not associate with anyone who was not diseased. That meant no family contacts, no hugging the kids or grandkids. That meant the leper could not go to worship God with other believers. Worst of all, the victim was often treated as a sinner, somehow deserving this cursed fate.

All sin looks this way to God.

> *Behold, the Lord's hand is not shortened, that it cannot save; nor His ear heavy, that it cannot hear. But your iniquities have separated you from your God; and your sins have hidden His face from you, so that He will not hear (Isaiah 59:1-2).*

God wants to save man, wants to be near man—but God keeps man at a distance because of sin. You might think your "little" sin is no big deal. But to God *all* sin is ugly. To God, sin in any form is disgusting.

Sadly, all of us have come down with the disease called sin.

> *There is none righteous, no, not one...all have sinned and fall short of the glory of God (Rom. 3:10, 23).*

Every one of us looks ugly before God, just as ugly as any leper would look to us. We cannot look down on those whose ugliness is different than ours. We cannot pretend our particular disease is better than someone else's. We are all sinners, and we all look ugly to God.

Compassion Moves God

The leper chose to come to Jesus. Jesus had already begun His public ministry and word of His power to heal had spread. The leper probably thought he had nothing to lose and everything to gain, so he obediently approached Jesus. We know he trusted Jesus to do something for him, he had faith. We know he was obedient as he would not approach Jesus too closely so as to cause Him to become unclean.

Jesus was filled with compassion. He cared for this poor man who had suffered from this disease. Jesus looked beyond the ugliness that was there and saw the human being underneath. Jesus could not stand by and let leprosy win this battle. Jesus acted out of compassion.

That is the nature of God. God reaches out to sinners like us because He loves us, ugliness and all.

> *For God so loved the world that He gave His only begotten Son, that whoever believes in Him should not perish but have everlasting life (John 3:16).*

The nature of God moves Him to reach out to us, just as Jesus reached out to the leper. God does this, in spite of how ugly our sin looks to Him.

> *But God demonstrates His own love toward us, in that while we were still sinners, Christ died for us (Rom. 5:8).*

Never doubt how much God loves you. He is willing to reach out to sinners like you and me and save us, in spite of our failures, our mistakes, our sins.

God Gives More Than We Ask

Jesus does an interesting thing with this leper.

> *And moved with compassion, He stretched out His hand, and touched him, and said to him, 'I am willing; be cleansed" (Mark 1:41).*

Jesus healed the man, but first the Master touched the man. How long had it been since anyone had touched him? How long had he gone without any human contact of any kind? Whatever the status of his disease, the leper felt the touch of a human hand for the first time in a long time.

Jesus runs a risk in touching the man. According to the law He would be unclean if He touched a leper. But Jesus looked beyond the man's obvious physical need for healing. The Lord saw the man's need for human contact, for acceptance, for love. So, before He healed the man, Jesus touched Him. Jesus knew the man's need better than the man himself.

So it is with us. Jesus knows we need to be forgiven. But He knows much more than that. He knows we need to get along. He knows we need love and acceptance. So the Lord reaches out to us as well, even while we are unclean. He loves us Himself, and places us in a body of believers who will also love us.

> *Beloved, let us love one another, for love is of God; and everyone who loves is born of God and knows God. He who does not love does not know God, for God is love. In this the love of God was manifested toward us, that God has sent His only begotten Son into the world, that we might live through Him. In this is love, not that we loved God, but that He loved us and sent His Son to be the propitiation for our sins. Beloved, if God so loved us, we also ought to love one another (1 John 4:7-11).*

God looks beyond the surface requests we make of Him and gives us more than we can imagine.

> *Now to Him who is able to do exceedingly abundantly above all that we ask or think, according to the power that works in us, to Him be glory in the church by Christ Jesus to all generations, forever and ever (Eph. 3:20-21).*

How that leper must have felt to have a human hand on him. You and I can only imagine how good it will be when God reaches out to us and gives us more than we can ask or think.

The Clean Cry Out

Jesus tells the leper to follow the Law of Moses, go show himself to a priest who will examine him to see if he is clean. Then the former leper would be admitted back into society, back into his home and family, back into the congregation of believers. Jesus also tells the man to keep this private, to tell no one.

But the man has experienced too much blessing to be quiet. He spread the news. What a story he must have told, how Jesus not only healed him, but this new teacher reached out to him and touched him as he was healed. Jesus may have wanted the man to keep it private, but the man had been given too much. He spread the news around.

That is what happens when people meet Jesus. They cannot keep quiet. When we realize the ugliness is gone, we want to tell others. When we feel the touch of God and the blessings he gives beyond what we expect, we want to tell others. As God reclaims sinners, it is a natural process that they will want to tell others the story of their cleansing.

> *Oh, give thanks to the Lord, for He is good! For His mercy endures forever. Let the redeemed of the Lord say so, whom He has redeemed from the hand of the enemy (Psalm 107:1-2).*

Be Cleansed and Cry Out

I want to invite you to come to Jesus for cleansing today. Put your faith in Him, recognizing that only He has the power to cleanse you. Turn from the ugliness of your sin, and then let Jesus cleanse you with His blood as you are baptized into His death and rise to walk in newness of life (Rom. 6:3-4). Then, with other believers, you can begin to tell the story of the day Jesus touched you.

WE ARE GOD'S FELLOW-WORKERS

So then neither he who plants is anything, nor he who waters, but God who gives the increase. Now he who plants and he who waters are one, and each one will receive his own reward according to his own labor. For we are God's fellow workers; you are God's field, you are God's building (1 Cor. 3:7-9).

One of the most sublime and glorious privileges to be found in the Christian life is that of working together with God. Being "fellow-workers" with God simply means that we are working with God and He is working with us, that we are partners.

The apostle Paul wrote,

We then, as workers together with Him, also plead with you not to receive the grace of God in vain. For He says: "In an acceptable time I have heard you, and in the day of salvation I have helped you." Behold, now is the accepted time; behold, now is the day of salvation (2 Cor. 6:1-2).

The fact that God is pleased with this partnership arrangement is shown from His own part in it:

And they went out and preached everywhere, the Lord working with them and confirming the word through the accompanying signs (Mark 16:20).

The apostle Paul wrote of his own life,

I have been crucified with Christ; it is no longer I who live, but Christ lives in me (Gal. 2:20).

That is real partnership! That enabled that great apostle to write later,

It is God who works in you both to will and to do for His good pleasure ... I can do all things through Christ who strengthens me (Phil. 2:13; 4:13).

God worked through Moses to lead Israel out of Egypt (Acts 7:35-36; 13:16-17). He worked through the young man David to slay the Philistine giant, Goliath (1 Sam. 17:37). In a similar way, God still works through His people today.

Working Together With God

Although God has infinite power, still He has always shared with man the fellowship of joint effort. When man was placed in the Garden of Eden, he still worked with God. After all things were created and furnished for man, *"Then the Lord God took the man and put him in the garden of Eden to tend and keep it"* (Gen. 2:15). God could have done it, but He gave the job to man. In a similar vein, God gave Noah the work of building the ark (Gen. 6). Again, God could have done it by Himself, but he chose Noah to be His "fellow-worker" in the project. We could also recall the examples of Caleb, Ezra, Nehemiah, Daniel, Elijah, and dozens of other Old Testament characters who acted in partnership with God.

A simple truth that has often been stated and demonstrated is this: "God will not do for man that which man is able to do for himself." When Jesus performed His first miracle, turning water into wine at the wedding feast in Cana, He gave men something to do: *"Fill the waterpots with water"* (John 2:7). Christ allowed another to furnish the loaves and fishes which were to become a feast for five thousand men (Matt. 14:13-21). In order to convince the disciples on the sea of Galilee, the Lord provided (miraculously) *"a multitude of fish"* (John 21:6). But first, the Lord told them, *"Cast the net on the right side of the boat."* Partnership—there was something for them to do to enjoy the Lord's blessing.

Partnership in Becoming a Child of God

We must not overlook that even in becoming a child of God, one is working in partnership with God. As Paul wrote,

> *For by grace you have been saved through faith, and that not of yourselves; it is the gift of God (Eph. 2:8).*

Notice that carefully: it is by grace (God's part) through faith (man's part) that we are saved. There, again, is the partnership—we are "workers together with God."

In hearing the word of the Lord, faith is produced by a willing acceptance of the stated facts of the gospel. God delivered His word by the Holy Spirit who guided the apostles *"into all the truth"* (John 16:13), so that what they preached and wrote was literally *"the word of God"* (1 Cor. 2:11-13; 1 Thes. 2:13). We hear that word, and accept it, by faith, as the rule for our lives. Paul wrote,

> *Or do you despise the riches of His goodness, forbearance, and longsuffering, not knowing that the goodness of God leads you to repentance? (Rom. 2:4).*

And so, "by faith," we are led to repent of our sins and submit to God's will for our lives.

When one is led by the Lord to trust Him for salvation, he is like those on Pentecost who then asked, "What shall we do?" God, by the mouth of the apostle Peter answered,

> *Repent, and let every one of you be baptized in the name of Jesus Christ for the remission of sins ... Then those who gladly received his word were baptized; and that day about three thousand souls were added to them"* (Acts 2:38, 41).

There was no quibbling—they just did what God told them to do! Partnership, "workers together with God."

Jesus had promised, *"He who believes and is baptized will be saved"* (Mark 16:16), so that faith *"works through love"* (Gal. 5:6). The apostle Paul shows that we must die to sin, be buried with Christ in baptism and be raised to walk in newness of life (Rom. 6:3-4). It is faith that leads sinners to obey the Lord in baptism:

> *Having been buried with Him in baptism, in which you also were raised with Him through faith in the working of God, who raised Him from the dead"* (Col. 2:12).

Thus, in every step of the path toward salvation in Christ (Rom. 6:3-6), we are "working together with God."

"To Seek and to Save the Lost"

When one is led by faith to be *"baptized into Jesus Christ,"* he is then a child of God (Gal. 3:26-27). And, "in Christ," again one becomes a fellow-worker with God. We must keep in mind that God uses no hands to minister to those in need, except ours. He uses our feet to run His errands of mercy. And He must employ our tongues to tell of the wonders of His love for lost sinners. When we walk in paths of righteousness, when we give ourselves in benevolent care, when we speak of His glory—in all of this we are "workers together with God."

If we will fully accept the divine import of this partnership, we will certainly heed His admonition to:

> *Go into all the world and preach the gospel to every creature. He who believes and is baptized will be saved; but he who does not believe will be condemned (Mark 16:15-16).*

Jesus stated clearly His mission:

> *For the Son of Man has come to seek and to save that which was lost (Luke 19:10).*

If we are "workers together with God," that is also our mission in this life.

After God had given His Son to die for sinful man, the gospel was placed in the hands of men for distribution to all the lost of all the world. God no longer used angels, nor spoke directly to man. From the beginning of the New Covenant, God has never altered the procedure by which sinners have revealed to them the terms of salvation. It has always been the gospel preached from the lips of men—never directly from God or angels!

As the apostle Paul stated it,

> *For it is the God who commanded light to shine out of darkness, who has shone in our hearts to give the light of the knowledge of the glory of God in the face of Jesus Christ. But we have this treasure in earthen vessels, that the excellence of the power may be of God and not of us (2 Cor. 4:6-7).*

Thus God works through us to set forth His marvelous grace to sinful man. The treasure of the gospel of salvation is in earthen vessels, and in our using the gospel to save the lost, we are "workers together with God."

God works in us to reconcile the world to Himself:

> *Therefore, if anyone is in Christ, he is a new creation; old things have passed away; behold, all things have become new. Now all things are of God, who has reconciled us to Himself through Jesus Christ, and has given us the ministry of reconciliation, that is, that God was in Christ reconciling the world to Himself, not imputing their trespasses to them, and has committed to us the word of reconciliation. Now then, we are ambassadors for Christ, as though God were pleading through us: we implore you on Christ's behalf, be reconciled to God (2 Cor. 5:17-20).*

As we preach the gospel, we are "workers together with God."

The Growth of the Church

Our close cooperation with God is shown again in Paul's words, *"I planted, Apollos watered, but God gave the increase"* (1 Cor. 3:6). As Paul preached the gospel, he planted the *"seed of the kingdom"* (Luke 8:11). As Apollos followed Paul in Corinth, and preached the same gospel to those new Christians, he watered the seed. And so it is today. God works through our efforts to reach the lost with the gospel. God still "works in you" to accomplish His purpose in reaching the lost with the saving gospel of Christ.

The place of our work is shown:

> *Whoever calls on the name of the Lord shall be saved. How then shall they call on Him in whom they have not believed? And how shall they believe in Him of whom they have not heard? And how shall they hear without a preacher? And how shall they preach unless they are sent? As it is written: 'How beautiful are the feet of those who preach the gospel of peace, who bring glad tidings of good things!' (Rom. 10:13-15).*

The treasure is in earthen vessels, and to effect the salvation of those in sin, the earthen vessels must pour out the story of God's redeeming love. Thereby we become "workers together with God" in saving the lost.

Doesn't it thrill you to know that God, your Father, is your partner in your spiritual endeavors? We can tell the whole world of the glory of God, His goodness, His wisdom, His purity, His love, and His compassion. When we do that, we can glory in the fact that because of His love, we are the "children of God" (1 John 3:1). And, as the children of God, we are then "workers together with God."

FALSE TEACHERS – WHO ARE THEY?

The question has been raised, "False teachers, who are they?" This question suggests that it is possible to give the names of those who are false teachers. While this is a possibility, some adamantly oppose the idea of charging an individual by name as a false teacher. Not only are we allowed to identify false teachers, we are commanded to do so.

> *Now I urge you, brethren, note those who cause divisions and offenses, contrary to the doctrine which you learned, and avoid them (Romans 16:17).*

The word "note (or mark)" indicates a "warning against those who cause divisions." While it is not the only thing that causes division, teaching false doctrine obviously does so. Paul named Hymenaeus and Philetus who were propagating false doctrine concerning the resurrection,

> *But shun profane and idle babblings, for they will increase to more ungodliness. And their message will spread like cancer. Hymenaeus and Philetus are of this sort, who have strayed concerning the truth, saying that the resurrection is already past; and they overthrow the faith of some (2 Timothy 2:16-18).*

A common belief is that what makes a false teacher is not so much his teaching, but his character. It is true that often a false teacher has serious character flaws. The various scandals that arise among "televangelists" show that many of these are not people of pristine character. Truly, they personify Paul's statement that some are "*destitute of the truth, who suppose that gain is godliness*" (1 Timothy 6:5). One verse earlier, Paul wrote that one who teaches contrary to sound doctrine is "proud" (v. 4). This may explain why one would continue to hold to his falsehood when confronted with its error.

By contrast, when Aquila and Priscilla helped Apollos see his error, he immediately corrected his teaching.

> *Now a certain Jew named Apollos, born at Alexandria, an eloquent man and mighty in the Scriptures, came to Ephesus. This man had been instructed in the way of the Lord; and being fervent in spirit, he spoke and taught accurately the things of the Lord, though he knew only the baptism of John. So he began to speak boldly in the synagogue. When Aquila and Priscilla heard him, they took him aside and explained to him the way of God more accurately (Acts 18:24-26).*

The Bible reveals some of the flawed motives of false teachers. Paul spoke of those who "*teach things which they ought not, for the sake of dishonest gain*" (Titus 1:11). Peter compared false teachers with Balaam, "*who loved the wages of unrighteousness*" (2 Peter 2:15). Jude spoke of those who "*reject authority, and speak evil of dignitaries*" (Jude 8). Peter tied this attitude together with presumption and self-will (2 Peter 2:10).

But, the danger of a false teacher is not the quality of his character; it is the content of his message. We may not be able to determine whether a teacher's heart is right, but still we can be deceived by his message. Even if he is sincere in his proclamation of error, that error is still harmful.

Paul mentioned some who preach the truth with wrong motives—envy and strife—and without condoning the attitudes, he rejoiced that truth was preached,

> *Some indeed preach Christ even from envy and strife, and some also from goodwill: The former preach Christ from selfish ambition, not sincerely, supposing to add affliction to my chains; but the latter out of love, knowing that I am appointed for the defense of the gospel. What then? Only that in every way, whether in pretense or in truth, Christ is preached; and in this I rejoice, yes, and will rejoice (Philippians 1:15-18).*

Let it be clearly understood that what makes a person a false teacher is that he teaches false doctrine.

False teachers—who are they? They are those who have strayed from the truth. Paul asserted that Hymenaeus and Philetus were teachers *"who have strayed concerning the truth, saying that the resurrection is already past; and they overthrow the faith of some"* (2 Timothy 2:18). Strayed here is also translated as "erred" and means to deviate from anything, to miss the mark. The word does not reveal whether this deviation is intentional. The example of Apollos illustrates that one can do so unintentionally.

While it is true that one is of questionable character that intentionally teaches falsehood, as far as the effect on others is concerned, the teacher's motive does not matter. Whether Hymenaeus and Philetus knew that their teaching was in error did not change the fact that it overturned the faith of some.

False teachers—who are they? They are those who have twisted the scriptures. Peter said of Paul,

> *As also in all his epistles, speaking in them of these things, in which are some things hard to understand, which untaught and unstable people twist to their own destruction, as they do also the rest of the Scriptures (2 Peter 3:16).*

The idea is that the things taught within the epistles are perverted or twisted to make them appear to teach something that the Biblical writers never intended. Unlike the word "err" or "stray" in 2 Timothy 2:18, this word implies that some are dishonest with the scriptures. Rather than allowing the scriptures to speak for themselves, they will twist them into compliance with their self-chosen opinions.

Note further that even though these individuals are "untaught and unstable," God still holds them responsible for their actions. Whereas in 2 Timothy 2:18 it is the faith of the hearer that is overthrown, here it is the demise of the false teacher that is considered in the phrase *"to their own destruction."*

False teachers—who are they? They are those who teach "destructive heresies." Peter compared them with the false prophets of old.

> *But there were also false prophets among the people, even as there will be false teachers among you, who will secretly bring in destructive heresies, even denying the Lord who bought them, and bring on themselves swift destruction (2 Peter 2:1).*

Their methods are deceitful and their message is damnable. This passage illustrates that the problem is not just with the character of the teacher. The teaching itself is "damnable." False teaching brings swift destruction on both the teacher and the hearer.

How Can We Know Whether a Person is a False Teacher?

No false teacher identifies himself as such. To make the correct identification we must know the scriptures. We must try the spirits (principles—cf. 1 John 4:1) and we must compare what is taught with what is written (Acts 17:11).

> *The gospel of Christ ... is the power of God to salvation (Romans 1:16).*

> *The holy scriptures ...are able to make you wise for salvation (2 Timothy 3:15).*

> *All Scripture is given by inspiration of God, and is profitable for doctrine, for reproof, for correction, for instruction in righteousness, that the man of God may be complete, thoroughly equipped for every good work (2 Timothy 3:16, 17).*

God's Word contains "*all things that pertain to life and godliness*" (2 Peter 1:3). When observing these passages, the all-sufficiency of the soul-saving Word of God is evident. So, diligent study of the Scriptures will greatly aid any Christian in securing their hearts. That diligence will assist us in our effort to recognize and note the false teachers about us.

Form of Godliness, But No Power

The central landmark in all of man's history is the cross of Jesus Christ. It was foretold in the first prophecy of the Bible (Gen. 3:15) and is the basis of the Bible's last book. The cross epitomizes the love of God for lost sinners, and pictures His great desire to save us. The cross stands as the separation point between the Old Testament and the New, for the Old Law was *"nailed to his cross"* (Col. 2:14). And it was by the blood He shed there that Jesus became *"the mediator of a new covenant"* (Heb. 9:15). It was on that cross that Jesus Christ, the Son of God, having fulfilled the former testament (the Law of Moses), died in seeming humiliation and shame. As Paul wrote,

> *Christ has redeemed us from the curse of the law, having become a curse for us: for it is written, Cursed is every one that hangs on a tree (Gal. 3:13).*

The apostle Paul elsewhere wrote,

> *But know this, that in the last days perilous times will come: For men will be lovers of themselves, lovers of money, boasters, proud, blasphemers, disobedient to parents, unthankful, unholy, unloving, unforgiving, slanderers, without self-control, brutal, despisers of good, traitors, headstrong, haughty, lovers of pleasure rather than lovers of God, having a form of godliness but denying its power. And from such people turn away (2 Tim 3:1-5).*

These people are not totally irreligious—they hold to a "form of godliness." But they have "denied the power thereof." That is still a problem today.

The Power of the Cross

There are many who wear a gold cross on a chain around their necks, but deny by their lives what that symbol represents. The cross of Christ was set against a dark background. At Golgotha, "the place of a skull" (Matt. 27:33), with the rabble railing on Him and thieves on either side *"reviled Him with the same thing"* (Matt. 27:44), Jesus willingly gave up His life for others. As the jeweler displays his gems against the black cloth to better show, by contrast, their beauty and value, even so the death of Christ exemplifies the preciousness of the Son of God, being set against the black background of man's inhuman treatment.

The cross was rough and cruel. The earth was darkened while God's Son hung on that cross, and the earth shook. The whole world trembled beneath the weight of divine atonement as the Son of God died for mankind. The eyes of all spectators were focused on the One who died there, not on the cross itself. And even today, our thoughts should be on His death on the cross—that shows the love of God and His desire to save sinners—not simply on some golden ornament!

Whereas the burial place of Moses was kept a secret by God, lest his followers should enshrine it, the cross of Christ stands forth in bold relief that all mankind, throughout history, may view it from afar. Yet God's picture of the cross was not such as to cause thinking men to memorize—or idolize—the cross. Instead, God's emphasis is on the event transpired there.

The Preaching of the Cross

The Scripture says:

> *For the message of the cross is foolishness to those who are perishing, but to us who are being saved it is the power of God. For it is written: "I will destroy the wisdom of the wise, and bring to nothing the understanding of the prudent..." But we preach Christ crucified, to the Jews a stumbling block and to the Greeks foolishness, but to those who are called, both Jews and Greeks, Christ the power of God and the wisdom of God (1 Cor 1:18-24).*

The word of the cross is "the power of God," but that power can be thwarted by accepting and following worldly wisdom. In other words, such a life has *"a form of godliness, but has denied the power thereof."*

There are many religious people who place a likeness of the cross upon the spires of their church buildings, emblazon it on their possessions, make it prominent on their letterheads and even wear it as jewelry—and yet deny the very essence of its power. The death of Christ and the cross of Christ are used interchangeably in the Scriptures. The apostle Peter wrote of Jesus:

> *...who Himself bore our sins in His own body on the tree, that we, having died to sins, might live for righteousness (1 Pet. 2:24).*

Now notice that: Christ bore our sins on "the tree" (the cross). And Paul writes that:

> *...we were reconciled to God through the death of his Son (Rom. 5:10).*

Thus, we find that we are saved from sins, and reconciled to God, by the death of Christ on the cross. There is power in the cross, because there is power in the blood.

> *You were not redeemed with corruptible things, like silver or gold, from your aimless conduct received by tradition from your fathers, but with the precious blood of Christ, as of a lamb without blemish and without spot" (1 Pet. 1:18-19).*

How We Are Saved By The Cross

But how can we reach this cross for the benefits of the death of Jesus Christ? Herein lies the mistake of many who deny the power of the cross while holding to its form. Listen to God's word:

> *Or do you not know that as many of us as were baptized into Christ Jesus were baptized into His death? Therefore we were buried with Him through baptism into death, that just as Christ was raised from the dead by the glory of the Father, even so we also should walk in newness of life. For if we have been united together in the likeness of His death, certainly we also shall be in the likeness of His resurrection, knowing this, that our old man was crucified with Him, that the body of sin might be done away with, that we should no longer be slaves of sin (Rom 6:3-6).*

In the verses preceding, the inspired apostle had shown that we are *"Justified by his blood ... reconciled to God through the death of his Son"* (Rom. 5:9-10). Now, in Romans 6, he shows that we are *"baptized into his death."* That person who has not yet been baptized into Christ has not been baptized into His death. For such a person to wear the cross as an ornament is to hold to a vain "form of godliness" while denying the very power of the cross to save.

The apostle Paul also shows, in this same chapter, that when we *"obey from the heart the form of teaching"* (Rom. 6:17), we are *"made free from sin"* (v. 18). That "form of teaching" he has already shown to be the death, burial, and resurrection of Christ. We obey the "form of teaching" when we are "baptized into His death…buried with him through baptism" and then are "raised to walk in newness of life" (v. 3-4). To sing of "The Old Rugged Cross" while refusing to be baptized into the death of Christ is to deny the power of the cross.

Raised to Walk in Newness of Life

Notice again that God tells us that, when we are *"buried in baptism,"* we then are *"raised to walk in newness of life"* (Rom. 6:4). The purpose of our death and burial is that a new creature might live. The Bible says plainly,

> *Therefore, if anyone is in Christ, he is a new creation; old things have passed away; behold, all things have become new (2 Cor. 5:17).*

Professing to be Christian while still following after the lusts of the flesh is denying the power of the cross. We must be raised from baptism to become "new creatures in Christ," or else we are only holding to a "form of godliness, but denying the power thereof." As Jesus put it

> *If any man come after me, let him deny himself, take up his cross and follow me (Matt. 16:24).*

No greater vanity is shown in religion than that depicted by wearing a cross as an ornament, or making "the sign of the cross," and then turning to buy or participate in indulgences to gratify the lusts of basic carnality. Such corruption could stem only from a religion that vainly holds to a form of godliness but denies the real power of the cross. The true disciple of Jesus will say with Paul,

> *But God forbid that I should boast except in the cross of our Lord Jesus Christ, by whom the world has been crucified to me, and I to the world (Gal. 6:14).*

The same apostle also warned about some, even among the followers of Christ, who were "enemies of the cross of Christ."

> *For many walk, of whom I have told you often, and now tell you even weeping, that they are the enemies of the cross of Christ (Phil. 3:18).*

If you have not been baptized into Christ Jesus, you have not as yet reached the power of His death. If that is true, the cross is of "none effect" to you. Commit yourself with the whole heart to the Lord, be baptized into His death to reach the blood which cleanses you from sin and sets your feet upon the paths of "newness of life." Then, as a new creature, daily crucify the "old man of sin," living with power the Christian life. Don't deny the power of the cross, instead, willingly submit yourself to it.

Blessed Are The Peacemakers

Controversy seems to abound in our world; whether it is political and public, controversy such as an impeachment, or whether it is personal, such as a divorce. Disagreements and arguments seem to be everywhere.

Some people seek wisdom to overcome these controversies. The assumption is, that if we just knew enough or heard the right evidence we would all agree. But that hardly settles controversy. The O.J. Simpson trials prove this, as one jury found him not guilty and the other found him responsible for two deaths. And still there is tension and controversy around both of his trials and his life since.

James, the Lord's brother, wrote his letter during a time of controversy. He probably wrote early in the New Testament age, with some scholars contending that his was the first epistle written. If so, he wrote during a time of intense controversy among Christians. Some contended that all Gentiles must be circumcised to be Christians (Acts 15). Paul and Barnabas sharply disputed this, and church leaders gathered in Jerusalem to discuss the matter. James, perhaps writing in the midst of this controversy, has some interesting things to say about real wisdom and the peace that comes from wisdom. Look at what James gives us in chapter 3:13-18.

> *Who is wise and understanding among you? Let him show by good conduct that his works are done in the meekness of wisdom. But if you have bitter envy and self-seeking in your hearts, do not boast and lie against the truth. This wisdom does not descend from above, but is earthly, sensual, demonic. For where envy and self-seeking exist, confusion and every evil thing are there. But the wisdom that is from above is first pure, then peaceable, gentle, willing to yield, full of mercy and good fruits, without partiality and without hypocrisy. Now the fruit of righteousness is sown in peace by those who make peace.*

James discusses a wisdom that is based on a lifestyle, not on knowledge or experience. James says this wisdom creates peace and leads to righteousness. James doesn't say wisdom is found in settling all of our disagreements. Wisdom is not even found in resolving all controversies. Instead, wisdom is demonstrated in a life that reflects a Christ-like attitude. How can we develop the wisdom James says will lead to peace?

Confront the Attitudes Within

The first thing we can do is confront the attitudes within. James tells us about the wisdom of the world. That wisdom is full of jealousy, arrogance and selfish ambition. When you face controversy, the first place to go is inside your own heart to be sure that your motives are pure. Too often when we must face disagreements, we are worried about proving how smart we are. Or, we are trying to show others *we* have the answer—that is, our pride gets in the way. Then, the controversy is worsened as disagreements turn into battles which turn into wars. That is James' point. When we use earthly wisdom, we get caught up in disorder and every evil practice. People who have good intentions, but fail to confront the attitude within, often cause more problems because of the tone they take in the middle of controversy.

When we fail to confront the attitudes within, we go into battle unprepared. This is true even if the controversy is merely a matter of opinion, such as when to have worship services. Sadly, I have seen and heard of more churches disrupted over opinions than anything else. Always this was because someone or other wanted to prove how "wise" they were and insisted on getting their way. Using worldly wisdom, disorder followed, and people who were not evil got caught up in all kinds of evil practices.

But we must confront the attitudes within even if the battle is over something serious, such as instrumental music. Even when the stakes are high and doctrinal purity is at risk, we must start by going into our hearts to clear out the worldliness. James knows that being right on doctrine, and wrong in our attitudes or actions, means our doctrine will lose credibility. Who are the wise? The spiritually wise are those who look into their own hearts before trying to resolve simple or serious differences. We must check and confront our attitudes within.

Consider Others First

In order to gain wisdom that leads to peace, we must consider others first. In contrast to the wisdom of the world, James points us to a wisdom that has several characteristics. The interesting thing about all of these qualities is that they have to do with how we treat people. So, we are to be pure, that is set apart and holy in our actions. If we are truly wise, even when we are in controversy, we will not let Satan get a foot hold by caving in and using worldly methods. This would include ugly or cruel words. It would include hateful actions or statements. When we use such means we prove we are not wise.

Second, we are to be peaceable. Some people in the kingdom seem to be spoiling for a fight. They are ready to tackle and whip anyone over any issue. But James would say those kinds of people are not wise. They are worldly and will cause more division and evil, not less.

Third, we are to be gentle in our actions. Even if we are in disagreement over serious doctrinal issues, a truly wise Christian will be kind and gentle to those who disagree, even if they are wrong. That was how Jesus treated His opponents. That is how we should treat ours.

Fourth, we should be reasonable. This doesn't mean gullible, but it does mean open-minded. Those who disagree with me may be wrong, but perhaps I need to hear and understand what they are saying. Worldly wisdom is closed-minded. It already has all the facts and all the answers. The wisdom from above is reasonable. This means I consider the other person and their view point.

James also says we are to be full of mercy if we are wise. Think about this, for it is important. Who needs mercy? Those who are mistaken or even wrong. People who are without sin do not require mercy. So James is telling us that wise people know others may be mistaken or wrong, but still extend mercy and forgiveness to them. There is no room in Godly wisdom for holding grudges or an air of superiority. We are to be full of mercy.

James goes on to add we are to be without partiality. Other versions translate this as "unwavering," that is, not taking sides or entering the controversy with prejudice. It is the idea of standing solidly with fairness toward all parties. He concludes with the simple command to avoid hypocrisy.

James would not consider anyone wise who had not learned to clean up his own heart first and then treated others with respect and kindness, even if they disagreed. Anyone can get along with those who agree. The test of wisdom is what kind of person we are when we face controversy and disagreement.

Sow Peace

James finishes the passage by talking of sowing and harvesting. The seed to be sown is peace. When we face our own inner attitudes and then put others first, we are sowing peace among people. This allows us to keep discussion going. Jesus certainly demonstrated this quality in His life. How many times did He eat with Pharisees, talk with Pharisees, and even reach out to Pharisees in hopes of changing them? Jesus did this by using the kind of wisdom James has described. By sowing peace, Jesus laid a foundation for the later harvest.

This tells us something about our goals in controversial situations. Sometimes, we will not convince the other party of their error. But, by maintaining a Christ-like spirit, we can leave room for later discussions that may sway them. If we use worldly wisdom instead, we may convince them of our doctrine, but lose them due to our actions. So, when in the middle of controversy, sow peace. This is done with mercy, gentleness, and so on. When peace is sown, there is one inevitable result.

Reap Righteousness

How do we get people to do what is right? How can we persuade them or convince them they need to change? It starts by sowing peace, by demonstrating the attitudes James has described. When peace is sown, one result follows. The fruit is righteousness. The way to change and shape people is not by proving how smart we are and winning all the arguments. The way to shape people is to demonstrate genuine wisdom by our actions and words. James says that by sowing peace we will achieve righteousness in the harvest.

Of course, the hard part about a harvest is that it takes time. No one sows a seed on Monday and expects to be picking fruit on Tuesday. It won't happen in the spiritual world, either. As we contend for our opinions or for God's revealed will, let us sow peace, knowing that God will bless the seed we sow with a harvest of righteousness in our lives and in the lives of those with whom we interact. We are to sow peace, and wait for the harvest to come. God will provide that in due time.

Are You Wise

Too often we mistake wisdom for the ability to speak well or persuade. I find it interesting James leaves those qualities out of his definition of the wisdom from above. It is not based on our education, our I.Q., or even how much experience we have. Wisdom is based on how well we have learned to imitate the Christ who died for us. Are you wise? Do you still let selfish ambition and arrogance rule in your relationships? Or have you learned to be pure, gentle, merciful, and so on?

This is why God asks you to surrender your life to Him at the very beginning. Why are faith and repentance and baptism so important? Because they reflect one who has looked inside and found sin. Because they reflect one who wants to become more like Jesus. Because they show a surrender to God's way of doing things from the very start. Instead of arguing with God, surrender to Him today. Be baptized. Instead of proving to others how "wise" you are, start living the kind of life James describes and watch God bless your world with a harvest of righteousness.

"Are There Few That Be Saved?"

Let us begin this morning by taking a look at Luke 13:23-24,

> *Then one said to Him, "Lord, are there few who are saved?" And He said to them, "Strive to enter through the narrow gate, for many, I say to you, will seek to enter and will not be able."*

A reading similar to this is the one just read from Matt. 7:13-14,

> *Enter by the narrow gate; for wide is the gate and broad is the way that leads to destruction, and there are many who go in by it. Because narrow is the gate and difficult is the way which leads to life, and there are few who find it."*

One of the often repeated truths of the Bible is that few will be saved, and many shall be lost. When Jesus was asked the question in Luke 13:23, He answered plainly. But, in view of the graciousness of God's scheme of redemption, why are the many not saved? What can account for this multitude not entering in? Does the Bible present an answer? And if so, can we profit by knowing it?

This morning, I hope to give you some things to think about regarding the "many".

Many Are Lost from Lack of Knowledge

One of the principal causes for the many being unsaved is lack of knowledge of what God has commanded for our lives. How often it is that we are met with, "Oh, I just don't know enough about the Bible to discuss it with you, but I am satisfied with my religion." Yet we boast of living in a land of Bibles and religious freedom! It is a terrible thing to confess, but many people are willingly ignorant of the word of God. What a tragedy that people scorn the study of the one book that can affect their salvation, but spend countless hours in other frivolous behavior.

It was lack of sufficient knowledge of the will of God that caused Saul of Tarsus to persecute the way of Christ. Later he wrote that he was

> *...a blasphemer, a persecutor, and an insolent man; but I obtained mercy because I did it ignorantly in unbelief (1Tim. 1:13).*

But even though his lack of knowledge was a mitigating factor, he was still guilty and spoke of himself as being "*chief of sinners*" for those acts done in ignorance (1 Tim. 1:15).

Because of their lack of knowledge of the will of Christ, the Israelites were not saved. Instead, Paul wrote of them as follows,

> *Brethren, my heart's desire and prayer to God for Israel is that they may be saved. For I bear them witness that they have a zeal for God, but not according to knowledge. For they being ignorant of God's righteousness, and seeking to establish their own righteousness, have not submitted to the righteousness of God (Rom. 10:1-3).*

Here were sincere and honest people who were in error. Yes, one cause for the many being unsaved is a lack of knowledge. John 8:32 is very clear:

You shall know the truth, and the truth shall make you free.

Many Trust in Human Standards

Many remain unsaved because they have placed their trust in human standards. Often it is said, "I believe this will please God…" After a rambling definition of a personal philosophy, assurance is stated that as long as a person is sincere and honest, salvation is sure. But this deifies human wisdom into a god of our own fashioning. Just remember that the Wise Man said,

The way of a fool is right in his own eyes (Prov. 12:15).

The prophet spoke the truth when he said,

O Lord, I know the way of man is not in himself; It is not in man who walks to direct his own steps (Jer. 10:23).

Too many people are trying to guide themselves, or choose a guide, rather than accepting the guidance of God's word. When people seek to enter the church of their choice, choose a name to wear in religion or to formulate a plan for being saved, they are doomed to failure. God reserves the right to appoint doctrine, the church, the name, and the scheme of redemption for man. We can't alter a one of them.

It may seem, to some, better to circumvent God's established order, and make improvements on it. But this only portrays human folly. God has said,

"My thoughts are not your thoughts, Nor are your ways My ways," says the Lord. "For as the heavens are higher than the earth, So are My ways higher than your ways, And My thoughts than your thoughts" (Isa. 55:8-9).

It is foolish to seek improvements on that which is ordained of God. Isaiah could still speak to this people:

Just as they have chosen their own ways, And their soul delights in their abominations, So will I choose their delusions, And bring their fears on them; Because, when I called, no one answered, When I spoke they did not hear; But they did evil before My eyes, And chose that in which I do not delight (Isa. 64:3-4).

Many Love the Error in Religion

Many will be lost because they have a love for the error that binds them. Even when truth is clearly presented to them, they reject it and cling to the error. There have been statements made, "I would die and go to hell before I would accept that!" And they likely will, unless they change their attitude toward God's truth. God's prophet wrote,

An astonishing and horrible thing has been committed in the land: The prophets prophesy falsely, and the priests rule by their own power; and My people love to have it so. But what will you do in the end? (Jer. 5:30-31).

When people have a love for error, surely the truth can't free them.

> *For the time will come when they will not endure sound doctrine, but according to their own desires, because they have itching ears, they will heap up for themselves teachers; and they will turn their ears away from the truth, and be turned aside to fables (2 Tim. 4:3-4).*

This does not necessarily mean that all honesty and sincerity has fled. Further, they may sincerely believe lies and errors, after once having spurned the truth. Satan may then appear

> *...with all unrighteous deception among those who perish, because they did not receive the love of the truth, that they might be saved. And for this reason God will send them strong delusion, that they should believe the lie, that they all may be condemned who did not believe the truth but had pleasure in unrighteousness (2 Thes. 2:10-12).*

Before anyone gets too satisfied with his/her religious affiliation, it might be well to thoroughly check it.

Independence and Stubbornness

There are many who are unsaved because they simply refuse to submit to God and stubbornly oppose making any confession of error. The prophet once said,

> *I listened and heard, but they do not speak aright. No man repented of his wickedness, saying, 'What have I done?' Everyone turned to his own course, as the horse rushes into the battle (Jer. 8:6).*

Conditions of today are very little different. It is still a rebellious people arrogantly opposing the words of the Lord. As Jeremiah called on his people to return to "*the old paths,*" they replied, "*We will not walk in it*" (Jer. 6:16).

The Jews crowded Christ with the following question,

> *"How long do You keep us in doubt? If You are the Christ, tell us plainly." Jesus answered them, "I told you, and you do not believe. The works that I do in My Father's name, they bear witness of Me." (John 10:24-25).*

It was not because of lack of evidence, but their own stubbornness that prevented their believing. It is also true of many people today. They reject plain commands of the Lord by dodging behind some passage where that command is NOT given. Stubbornness leads them to pursue a doctrine they now know to be in error, uphold a church nowhere mentioned in the Bible, and wear a name foreign to the one divinely given. "Death and destruction are in their going."

Love of Material Wealth

Love of material wealth has beguiled many who will not be saved. They have sold their birthright for less than a mess of meat. Heaven with all of its treasures is scorned by those who lavish all their efforts to follow and worship the god of gold. Men grow hard of heart and crusty of soul in the vain philosophy that success in life is measured in terms of dollars and cents. Paul wrote,

Command those who are rich in this present age not to be haughty, nor to trust in uncertain riches but in the living God, who gives us richly all things to enjoy (1 Tim. 6:17).

Earlier in that chapter, he had written,

But those who desire to be rich fall into temptation and a snare, and into many foolish and harmful lusts which drown men in destruction and perdition. For the love of money is a root of all kinds of evil, for which some have strayed from the faith in their greediness, and pierced themselves through with many sorrows (vs. 9-10).

In 2 Timothy 4:10 we read, *"Demas has forsaken me, having loved this present world."* But how many more names might be superimposed upon that of Demas today? Mankind has become infatuated with the world to the extent that God has been crowded out. Many will not be saved because they loved this present world, and the worldly riches it has to offer.

The Thief of Time

Possibly procrastination will account for the damnation of more people than any of the other hindrances mentioned in this lesson. It is so easy to let this "thief of time" steal away our days before we are aware. When Paul stood before the governor, making his defense, Felix, as he reasoned about righteousness, self-control, and the judgment to come, trembled and said,

Go away for now; when I have a convenient time I will call for you (Acts 24:25).

But Felix never found that convenient time for saving his soul. And since his day, myriads of people have offered the same excuse for not obeying their God. Good resolutions are always postdated. The intentions are the finest, but are to become effective at some later date. Time after time I have wondered how to impress this lesson upon those who attend the funeral of another, one who fully intended to become a child of God, but put it off just one day too many!

One of the saddest pictures presented in the album of God's book is in the language of Jeremiah 8:20,

The harvest is past, the summer has ended, and we are not saved!

Conclusion

Do you fall into one of these categories? Is it worth what it will cost your soul? Don't choose the broad way that leads to destruction. Be one of the few that will be saved.

What Is Happening to Us

A lack of scriptural emphasis will always bring chaos into our lives. Men have forgotten the Christ and the bulwark of righteousness which He provides. In Prov. 14:34, the inspired penman boldly affirmed this truth:

Righteousness exalts a nation, But sin is a reproach to any people.

We Americans desperately need to get back to the Bible teaching in our homes. For example, in 2017 this nation alone contributed approximately 1,000,000 divorces to an already degrading world scene.

God makes it abundantly clear,

For the Lord God of Israel says that He hates divorce (Mal. 2:16).

And Jesus said,

For this reason a man shall leave his father and mother and be joined to his wife, and the two shall become one flesh. So then, they are no longer two but one flesh. Therefore what God has joined together, let not man separate (Matt. 19:5-6).

But the lack of respect for God's will regarding marriage is only a symptom of the underlying lack of morality of the people of this nation.

We need to get back to Bible teaching regarding respect for authority. The Holy Scriptures inform us that we should pay our taxes (Matt. 22:21), obey our rulers (Rom. 13:1-7), and pray for those in authority (1 Tim. 2:1-2). This is the only way to stop the rioting, crime, and anarchy which plague our cities today. The Bible alone has the answer to our dilemma. As a result, we must have the courage to return to its sacred teachings.

You and I certainly need to return to God's word for moral purity and holiness. In an age of nudity, filth, and sensuality, all of us must return to the modesty, integrity, and spirituality of New Testament Christianity (Phil. 4:8). Church councils may sanction homosexual preachers, but the Bible very clearly and strongly rebukes such sinfulness. Paul wrote,

For this reason God gave them up to vile passions. For even their women exchanged the natural use for what is against nature. Likewise also the men, leaving the natural use of the woman, burned in their lust for one another, men with men committing what is shameful, and receiving in themselves the penalty of their error which was due (Rom. 1:26-27).

Also,

Do you not know that the unrighteous will not inherit the kingdom of God? Do not be deceived. Neither fornicators, nor idolaters, nor adulterers, nor homosexuals, nor sodomites, nor thieves, nor covetous, nor drunkards, nor revilers, nor extortioners will inherit the kingdom of God (1 Cor. 6:9-10).

The apostle Paul encourages us to moral purity with these words:

> *For the grace of God that brings salvation has appeared to all men, teaching us that, denying ungodliness and worldly lusts, we should live soberly, righteously, and godly in the present age" (Titus 2:11-12).*

It is long overdue, but still we plead for all men everywhere to return to the wholesome purity which Jesus stressed in the Sermon on the Mount: *"Blessed are the pure in heart, for they shall see God"* (Matt. 5:8).

Too many people are like the ones Macauley wrote of, "Who only have periodic bursts of morality," and therefore lead an uneven sojourn that is void of *"the peace of God which passes understanding"* (Phil. 4:7). This type of emphasis will never glorify God or magnify the Lord Jesus Christ. Paul, to the Christians in Philippi wrote,

> *According to my earnest expectation and hope that in nothing I shall be ashamed, but with all boldness, as always, so now also Christ will be magnified in my body, whether by life or by death (Phil. 1:20).*

One of the grandest and most eloquent of the benefits of moral purity is the fact that it puts us in the wonderful company of heroes of the faith. These are people *"Of whom the world was not worthy"* (Heb. 11:38). As Christians, we live *"in hope of eternal life"* (Titus 1:2), and yet, even here below, we bask in the sunlight of that vast host of faithful ones whose memorable deeds surround us and cheer us on to victory.

How can America be saved? Since Jehovah *"rules in the kingdoms of men"* (Dan. 4:25), and in His sight the nations are as *"the drop of a bucket"* (Isa. 40:15); if we are to preserve America, we must face up to our immediate responsibilities before our Creator. In one of the most familiar statements regarding national concern, James Russell Lowell declared:

> Once to every man and nation
> Comes the moment to decide;
> In the strife of truth and falsehood
> For the good or evil side.

An impartial appraisal of American degeneracy demands that godly citizens awaken, arise and meet the challenge before us. In 1940, in one of his famous "fireside chats," Franklin D. Roosevelt stated,

> We build and defend, not for our generation alone, we defend the foundations laid by our fathers. We build a way of life for generations yet unborn. We defend, and we build a way of life, not for America alone, but for all mankind.

Those who are even remotely conversant with the decline and fall of the Roman Empire can see the parallels of that society with our society in America today.

What can we do to stem the tide of reprehensible conduct that will eventuate in hell? The following are some suggestions for essential ingredients.

Godliness in our homes—The psalmist wrote, *"Unless the Lord builds the house, they labor in vain who build it"* (Psa. 127:1). Joshua said, *"But as for me and my house, we will serve the Lord"* (Josh. 24:15).

Since "*the house of the wicked shall be overthrown, but the house of the righteous shall stand*" (Prov. 12:7; 14:11), we need to seek God first in our homes (Matt. 6:33). We must build our homes on the love, faithfulness and compassion of Jesus Christ. We must have Godliness in our homes.

Respect for authority—"*There is no power but of God*" (Rom. 13:1), and we are told to "*obey them that have the rule over you*" (Heb. 13:17). We are told to pray for those who are in leadership and in rulership around the world; not just for our government leaders, but for the rulers of the whole world.

> *Therefore I exhort first of all that supplications, prayers, intercessions, and giving of thanks be made for all men, for kings and all who are in authority, that we may lead a quiet and peaceable life in all godliness and reverence (1 Tim. 2:1-2).*

Restore Bible preaching—Jesus told the apostles, "*Go into all the world and preach the gospel to every creature*" (Mark 16:15). The apostle Paul urgently exhorted the young Timothy, "*Preach the word, in season, out of season*" (2 Tim. 4:2). To Titus he wrote, "*Speak the things which are proper for sound doctrine*" (Titus 2:1), and Peter urges, "*If any man speak, let him speak as the oracles of God*" (1 Pet. 4:11).

Evangelistic zeal—We must return to evangelistic zeal. The great commission challenges Christians till the end of time to preach the saving gospel to a lost world (Mark 16:15). "*He that wins souls is wise*" (Prov. 11:30). This is God's salient reminder to all of us. It must grieve us when souls are lost, when people are "*as sheep not having a shepherd*" (Matt. 9:36). We should say in these circumstances, with the apostle Paul, "*Woe is me if I do not preach the gospel*" (1Cor. 9:16).

Personal purity of life—The Bible says,

> *Keep yourself pure ... Abstain from all forms of evil, cleave to that which is good, abhor that which is evil, depart from iniquity, think on things that are pure (Phil. 4:8).*

The real strength of America is neither its military might nor its economic base. The real power of America is her goodness. It is the doing of right, simply because it is right (Eph. 6:1). This is the real test of morality.

In the final analysis, the survival and salvation of any nation is based on the personal integrity of the individual citizens.

> *Righteousness exalts a nation, but sin is a reproach to any people (Prov. 14:34).*

This is God's brief, but eternal reminder to all of us that the moral integrity of any nation—from the rulers to the most humble citizen—is the basis on which God will bless and sustain any nation on this earth.

The apostle Paul wrote, "*Imitate me, just as I also imitate Christ*" (1 Cor. 11:1). As Peter wrote it,

For to this you were called, because Christ also suffered for us, leaving us an example, that you should follow His steps: Who committed no sin, nor was deceit found in His mouth (1 Pet. 2:21-22).

It is my belief that we need to work to bring America back into harmony with the will of God by bringing our own lives into harmony with His teachings and His will.

Receiving the Blessings of God

How do we receive the promised blessings of God? At what point, and on what conditions, do we receive God's blessings? There is probably more confusion in the religious world over those two questions than any others. Some contend that there is nothing at all for us to do, that God simply bestows His blessings unconditionally upon those He chooses. Others say we must earn His blessings either by our works or by our suffering for our sins. But what does the Bible say?

The apostle Paul wrote,

> *For by grace you have been saved through faith, and that not of yourselves; it is the gift of God, not of works, lest anyone should boast (Eph. 2:8-9).*

This passage makes it clear that we cannot *earn* God's blessings; that we cannot be saved by our own efforts. As a result, some contend that we must be saved by "faith only," that there are no other conditions. But the Bible answers that clearly:

> *What does it profit, my brethren, if someone says he has faith but does not have works? Can faith save him? ... Thus also faith by itself, if it does not have works, is dead ... Was not Abraham our father justified by works when he offered Isaac his son on the altar? Do you see that faith was working together with his works, and by works faith was made perfect? ... You see then that a man is justified by works, and not by faith only (James 2:14, 17, 21-22, 24).*

The only time "faith only" is found in the Bible, God tells us that we are NOT justified by "faith only." Frankly, I don't know why people don't believe God on this!

So, when do we receive God's promised blessings, and under what conditions? Let us look at three examples in the Old Testament to see how people received God's promised blessings, and then conclude with the New Testament. Even though the Old Testament was "nailed to the cross" (Col. 2:14), and we are not under its laws and rules, it is still important for us to study it. As Paul said,

> *For whatever things were written before were written for our learning, that we through the patience and comfort of the Scriptures might have hope (Rom. 15:4).*

The principles under which God gives His promised blessings to man are clearly revealed in these examples.

The Healing from the Fiery Serpents

The people of Israel had been disobedient, railing against God, His laws, and His chosen leader, Moses (Num. 21:5). God sent "fiery serpents" among them as punishment, and many of them died (v. 6). The people then came confessing their sin and asking for mercy. God promised to heal them:

> *Then the Lord said to Moses, 'Make a fiery serpent, and set it on a pole; and it shall be that everyone who is bitten, when he looks at it, shall live' (Num. 21:8).*

God offered healing, but it was not granted without conditions. He gave instructions of what they were to do: (a) Moses was to make a serpent (of brass) and set it on a pole in their midst, (b) Those who were bitten were to look on this brazen serpent.

The next step is clearly shown:

> *But without faith it is impossible to please Him, for he who comes to God must believe that He is, and that He is a rewarder of those who diligently seek Him (Heb. 11:6).*

No one ever received a promised blessing of God without faith. These Israelites had to trust God to heal them, and that meant accepting His method of cure.

But they were not cured when they believed, for a "dead faith" (that is, "faith without works"—James 2:17) cannot avail. It must be a faith that obeys what God says. The people of Israel were not healed when they believed, but when their faith led them to look upon the serpent. No one received the promised blessing of healing until they did what God told them to do! Notice this:

> *And so it was, if a serpent had bitten anyone, when he looked at the bronze serpent, he lived (Num. 21:9).*

Notice, then, the pattern:
1. God promised the blessing,
2. He gave instructions for the people to follow,
3. the people believed,
4. they did what God said,
5. and the blessing was given.

Conquering the City of Jericho

When Israel came into the promised land of Canaan, the first city they had to conquer was Jericho (Josh. 6). How could they do it? First, God promised it to them (v. 2), and then told them how:

> *See! I have given Jericho into your hand ... You shall march around the city, all you men of war; you shall go all around the city once. This you shall do six days. And seven priests shall bear seven trumpets of rams' horns before the ark. But the seventh day you shall march around the city seven times, and the priests shall blow the trumpets ... All the people shall shout with a great shout; then the wall of the city will fall down flat. And the people shall go up every man straight before him (Josh. 6:2-5).*

It took a lot of faith for these people to do as God said, for as a military maneuver, this plan just made no sense at all. But God would give the plan power when the people trusted Him enough to do what He said. They marched around the city in accord with God's instructions, and when they did what God said, the walls of Jericho fell down and the city was theirs.

Notice the pattern was the same as with the healing from the bites of the serpents.
1. God promised them the city,
2. He gave instructions on what to do,

3. they believed God,
4. they did what God told them,
5. and they received the promised blessing.

And, again, please note that they did not receive the promised blessing when they first believed. The blessing was not given until they *obeyed God's word*.

The Cleansing of Naaman, the Leper

Naaman was a General in the army of Syria, which had conquered Israel (2 Kings 5). But he was a leper. His wife's servant girl, an Israelite, had been taken captive, and told her mistress about a man in Israel who could heal Naaman. So Naaman came to Israel to consult with the prophet, Elisha.

And Elisha sent a messenger to him, saying, "Go and wash in the Jordan seven times, and your flesh shall be restored to you, and you shall be clean" (2 Kings 5:10).

But Naaman was angry, thinking that was "too simple." He even said the rivers back home were just as good as the Jordan. But his servant convinced him to do what God had said.

So he went down and dipped seven times in the Jordan, according to the saying of the man of God; and his flesh was restored like the flesh of a little child, and he was clean (2 Kings 5:14).

This example follows the same pattern as we have found before.
1. God promised the blessing of healing from the leprosy,
2. He gave instructions as to what must be done,
3. Naaman had to believe,
4. he did what God said,
5. and the promised blessing was then received.

Did Naaman receive the promised blessing when he first believed? Or did he receive it when he had dipped six times (partial obedience)? No, not until he had fully complied with what God required did Naaman receive the promised blessing.

New Testament Examples of Conversion

We are not under the laws of the Old Testament today. So, we are not told to make a brazen serpent; march thirteen times around a city, or go dip seven times in the River Jordan. But God has promised us the blessing of salvation or the forgiveness of our sins, in Christ. How do we receive that promised blessing? Let us look at some examples in the New Testament Scriptures.

"Therefore let all the house of Israel know assuredly that God has made this Jesus, whom you crucified, both Lord and Christ." Now when they heard this, they were cut to the heart, and said to Peter and the rest of the apostles, "Men and brethren,

what shall we do?" Then Peter said to them, "Repent, and let every one of you be baptized in the name of Jesus Christ for the remission of sins" (Acts 2:36-38).

Then Philip went down to the city of Samaria and preached Christ to them ... When they believed Philip as he preached the things concerning the kingdom of God and the name of Jesus Christ, both men and women were baptized (Acts 8:5,12).

The eunuch said, "See, here is water. What hinders me from being baptized?" Then Philip said, "If you believe with all your heart, you may." And he answered and said, "I believe that Jesus Christ is the Son of God." So he commanded the chariot to stand still. And both Philip and the eunuch went down into the water, and he baptized him (Acts 8:36-38).

"Sirs, what must I do to be saved?" So they said, "Believe on the Lord Jesus Christ, and you will be saved, you and your household." Then they spoke the word of the Lord to him and to all who were in his house. And he took them the same hour of the night and washed their stripes. And immediately he and all his family were baptized (Acts 16:30-33).

"Saul, Saul, why are you persecuting Me?" And he said, "Who are You, Lord?" Then the Lord said, "I am Jesus, whom you are persecuting ... Arise and go into the city, and you will be told what you must do" ... Ananias said ... "And now why are you waiting? Arise and be baptized, and wash away your sins, calling on the name of the Lord" (Acts 9:4-6; 22:16).

Notice in each one of the above examples of salvation the same pattern that we have seen before.
1. God promised salvation,
2. He gave instructions to be followed,
3. people believed,
4. they did what God said,
5. God saved them.

There was no deviation from that pattern. Nor does God deviate from that today. No one has ever received a promised blessing from God who did not follow the pattern above. That is why the apostle Peter said, *"You have purified your souls in obeying the truth"* (1 Pet. 1:22). It is why the apostle Paul wrote,

Though you were slaves of sin, yet you obeyed from the heart that form of doctrine to which you were delivered. And having been set free from sin, you became slaves of righteousness (Rom. 6:17-18).

Just as in the cases noted from the Old Testament (the serpents, Jericho, Naaman), God's promised blessings are given only when we hear His promise, heed His instructions, believe Him, and do what He says. That hasn't changed. Not one of those examples shows one saved by faith only. Each received salvation from sins when his faith led him to be baptized in obedience to God. No one receives His promised blessing at "the point of faith," but when that faith leads him to do what God says. As the Bible says,

> *Do you see that faith was working together with his works, and by works faith was made perfect (James 2:22).*
>
> *For in Christ Jesus neither circumcision nor uncircumcision avails anything, but faith working through love (Gal. 5:6).*

Do you want to begin receiving the blessings of God? Ephesians 1:3 says all spiritual blessings are in Christ. So to receive those spiritual blessings, you must be in Christ. Romans 6:3 says, *"Or do you not know that as many of us as were baptized into Christ Jesus were baptized into His death?"* We must be obedient to the will of God in order to receive His blessings. If we can help you with this in any way, let us know, we want to help.

No One Ever Spoke Like This Man

Jesus had gone up to Jerusalem for the Feast of Tabernacles, in spite of the fact that He knew *"the Jews sought to kill him"* (John 7:1-2, 10). As He taught the people, the hatred of the Jews only increased. Finally, when some began to say, *"This is the Christ"* (v. 31, 41), the Jewish leaders decided to take action. They sent officers to arrest Jesus and bring him before the High Council. When the officers returned empty-handed, the chief priests and Pharisees asked, *"Why did you not bring him?"* The officers replied very simply: *"No one ever spoke the way this man does"* (v. 46). Those officers had never heard anyone speak as Jesus did. Nor has anyone else on earth!

If we were to make a list of great orators, we might include such men as Patrick Henry, Daniel Webster, Wm. Jennings Bryan, Franklin D. Roosevelt, Winston Churchill. Depending on who is making the list, there might be many more. But none of the above can compare with Jesus: *"No one ever spoke like this man."* When Jesus read from Isa. 61 in the synagogue at Nazareth,

> *All bore witness to Him, and marveled at the gracious words which proceeded out of His mouth (Luke 4:22).*

When He was only twelve, Jesus was left behind in Jerusalem by his parents. He was in the temple talking with the learned scribes of the Jews, and:

> *All who heard Him were astonished at His understanding and answers (Luke 2:47).*

But the greatest compliment of all came from God:

> *This is my beloved Son, in whom I am well pleased; hear him (Matt. 17:5).*

No One Ever Had Such Knowledge

Jesus had knowledge of GOD that no one else has ever had.

> *In the beginning was the Word, and the Word was with God, and the Word was God. He was in the beginning with God ... And the Word became flesh, and dwelt among us (John 1:1-2, 14).*

Jesus had knowledge of God, because He had been with Him in the beginning! He said,

> *For I have come down from heaven, not to do My own will, but the will of Him who sent Me... As the Father knows Me, even so I know the Father; and I lay down My life for the sheep (John 6:38; 10:15).*

No one ever had such knowledge of God as Jesus did.

No one ever had such knowledge of MAN as the Lord Jesus had. Not only was Jesus *"with God"* in the beginning, but,

> *All things were made through Him, and without Him nothing was made that was made. In Him was life (John 1:3-4).*

When man was created, the Son of God was involved in that act of creation. It is no wonder, then, that the Bible says,

And had no need that anyone should testify of man, for He knew what was in man (John 2:25).

Jesus could see into the heart of men, "*Knowing their thoughts*" (Matt. 9:4).

Not only did Jesus know man because He had been "*with God, and was God*" (John 1:1), but also because He was fully a man.

> *Therefore, in all things He had to be made like His brethren, that He might be a merciful and faithful High Priest in things pertaining to God, to make propitiation for the sins of the people. For in that He Himself has suffered, being tempted, He is able to aid those who are tempted (Heb. 2:17-18).*

He experienced what we do: pain, temptation, betrayal, sorrow. No one ever knew mankind like Jesus.

No one ever had such knowledge of the past, present and future as Jesus. He was there "*in the beginning*" (John 1:1-2) when the heavens and earth were created (Gen. 1). He watched from heaven with the Father, as history unfolded. In the present,

> *There is no creature hidden from His sight, but all things are naked and open to the eyes of Him to whom we must give account (Heb. 4:13).*

He also knows the future, as is evident when you read His prophecies about the building of His church, the sending of the Holy Spirit to the apostles, His many descriptions of His return and the Day of Judgment.

No One Ever Had Such Authority

Many speakers are interesting, not because they are good speakers, but because they speak with authority on their subject. But no one ever had the kind of authority that Jesus did, and does. John declared,

> *All things were made through Him, and without Him nothing was made that was made (John 1:3).*

Again, we read that it was "*through him*" that the Father made the worlds (Heb. 1:2). Being the Son of God (John 3:16), it is clear we should listen to Him:

> *I have glorified You on the earth. I have finished the work which You have given Me to do. And now, O Father, glorify Me together with Yourself, with the glory which I had with You before the world was (John 17:4-5).*

After His death on the cross, and His resurrection from the dead, Jesus told the apostles, "*All authority has been given to me in heaven and on earth*" (Matt 28:18). Long before Jesus was born in Bethlehem, God had spoken of Him to Moses:

> *I will raise up for them a Prophet like you from among their brethren, and will put My words in His mouth, and He shall speak to them all that I command Him. And it shall be that whoever will not hear My words, which He speaks in My name, I will require it of him" (Deut. 18:18-19).*

Jesus referred to this prophecy when He said,

> *He who rejects Me, and does not receive My words, has that which judges him—the word that I have spoken will judge him in the last day (John 12:48).*

In that great day, when all will "give account to God," Jesus will be the judge!

> *For we must all appear before the judgment seat of Christ, that each one may receive the things done in the body, according to what he has done, whether good or bad (2 Cor. 5:10).*

The Jews long looked for "the Messiah" (or "Christ") to come, the prophet who would bring them deliverance. The Samaritan woman spoke of this, to which Jesus replied: *"I who speak to you am he"* (John 4:26). On trial before the Jewish council, He was asked, *"Are you the Christ?"* His reply was firm: *"Yes, it is as you say"* (Matt. 26:63-64). The apostle Peter, preaching to the Jews in Jerusalem after the death and resurrection of Jesus, said:

> *Therefore let all the house of Israel know assuredly that God has made this Jesus, whom you crucified, both Lord and Christ (Acts 2:36).*

That is why Paul wrote later that Jesus is *"the King of kings and Lord of lords"* (1 Tim. 6:15). No one ever had such authority as Jesus.

No One Ever Had Such Incentive

Jesus was never confused about why He had come into this world:

> *The Son of man came to seek and to save that which was lost (Luke 19:10).*

That is why He left heaven. He was foretold as *"the seed" of woman,"* who would overcome Satan (Gen. 3:15; Heb. 2:15). He was also *"the seed of Abraham"* in whom all families of the world would be blessed (Gen. 22:18; Gal. 3:8, 16). In fact, it is "in Christ" that God gives to us every spiritual blessing (Eph. 1:3). And all of this was *"according to the eternal purpose [of God] which he accomplished in Christ Jesus our Lord"* (Eph. 3:11).

When man became a sinner (Gen. 3), God purposed to save mankind through Jesus Christ. Man, by his sins, had separated himself from God (Isa. 59:1-2). So God promised a Savior:

> *"Behold, the days are coming," says the Lord, "That I will raise to David a Branch of righteousness; a King shall reign and prosper, and execute judgment and righteousness in the earth. In His days Judah will be saved, and Israel will dwell safely; now this is His name by which He will be called: THE LORD OUR RIGHTEOUSNESS" (Jer. 23:5-6).*

Before His birth, the angel told Joseph, regarding Mary,

> *She will bring forth a Son, and you shall call His name Jesus, for He will save His people from their sins (Matt. 1:21).*

Not only did Jesus accept the knowledge that He was to be the Savior of the world, He also knew that He was the ONLY Savior! He said,

I am the way, the truth, and the life. No one comes to the Father except through Me (John 14:6).

If anyone is going to be saved, it is going to be Jesus that saves them. The apostles also showed this clearly as they said of Jesus:

Nor is there salvation in any other, for there is no other name under heaven given among men by which we must be saved (Acts 4:12).

No one ever had the kind of incentive Jesus did. He said, *"The words that I speak to you are spirit, and they are life"* (John 6:63). That is why, when Jesus asked the apostles if they would depart from Him, they answered, *"Lord, to whom shall we go? You have the words of eternal life"* (v. 68).

Jesus had to speak, for:

Everyone who has heard and learned from the Father comes to Me (John 6:45).

The only way anyone can hear "from the Father," is to listen to Jesus, for He is God's spokesman. The apostle Paul wrote later,

For I am not ashamed of the gospel of Christ, for it is the power of God to salvation for everyone who believes (Rom. 1:16).

Jesus knew that the only way people could be saved was to hear and respond to His word. No one else has ever had that kind of incentive to speak! So, the Lord told the apostles before he departed this earth,

Go into all the world and preach the gospel to every creature. He who believes and is baptized will be saved; but he who does not believe will be condemned (Mark 16:15-16).

No one ever cared like Jesus. That was His incentive. He wanted people to be saved—that is why He willingly died on the cross. His compassion is shown during His ministry on earth:

And Jesus, when He came out, saw a great multitude and was moved with compassion for them, because they were like sheep not having a shepherd. So He began to teach them many things (Mark 6:34).

That passage shows His compassion and His desire for their salvation; so He spoke the saving word to them.

What is your attitude toward Him as you "hear Jesus" today? Jesus *"would have all men to be saved, and come to the knowledge of the truth"* (1 Tim. 2:4). He wants you to hear Him, as you would hear the Father. As He said to the apostles, when He empowered them to preach His message:

He who hears you hears Me, he who rejects you rejects Me, and he who rejects Me rejects Him who sent Me (Luke 10:16).

His message is the gospel of salvation.

Yes, we must conclude, as did those officers who were sent to arrest Him: "*No one ever spoke like this man.*" Therefore, make sure that you are hearing Him.

Do Not Be Conformed to this World

Let us begin by taking a look at Romans 12:1-2:

I beseech you therefore, brethren, by the mercies of God, that you present your bodies a living sacrifice, holy, acceptable to God, which is your reasonable service. And do not be conformed to this world, but be transformed by the renewing of your mind, that you may prove what is that good and acceptable and perfect will of God.

It is not unusual to hear someone use the apologetic statement, "Oh, he just hasn't been able to adjust himself to the world." It is usually spoken disparagingly. Now, that *could* really be a great compliment!

Jesus Christ spent all of His life on this earth **NOT** adjusting to the world. Not only did He not adjust to the world, He never tried. No adjustment was necessary, nor desired. Jesus stood apart from the world, and He offered no apology for refusing to conform to the world. He required the same of His followers, and told them,

The world cannot hate you, but it hates Me because I testify of it that its works are evil (John 7:7).

Later, in John 15:18-19, Jesus explained to the disciples,

If the world hates you, you know that it hated Me before it hated you. If you were of the world, the world would love its own. Yet because you are not of the world, but I chose you out of the world, therefore the world hates you.

If we will just conform to the world, then the world will accept us. But Jesus never did conform to the world, nor does He expect us to conform to it.

Love Not This World

Christ is looking today for people who will be Christians, people who will stand forth as unadjusted individuals in a sinful world. The apostle wrote,

Do not love the world or the things in the world. If anyone loves the world, the love of the Father is not in him. For all that is in the world—the lust of the flesh, the lust of the eyes, and the pride of life—is not of the Father but is of the world. And the world is passing away, and the lust of it; but he who does the will of God abides forever (1 John 2:15-17).

Jesus Christ knew that His true disciples would never become adjusted to the world in which they lived. The Lord warned clearly of this in John 15:19:

If ye were of the world, the world would love its own.

In other words, if we expect to get along with the world, it has to be on the world's terms. When we do that, we forsake the Lord. The standards of the world say it is fine to commit adultery, lie, get drunk, read and look at sexually explicit material, cuss and use vulgar language—and a host of other such things. While these things are accepted by the world, Christians are not to be conformed to the world. We are called to a higher standard of morality than that.

Seek the Things that Are Above

Those who have been "buried with Christ in baptism" (Rom. 6:3-4; Col. 2:12) are called to look beyond this world for ideals, focus, and hope. The Lord wasn't calling for us to conform to the world when He had Paul write in Colossians 3:1-5,

> *If then you were raised with Christ, seek those things which are above, where Christ is, sitting at the right hand of God. Set your mind on things above, not on things on the earth. For you died, and your life is hidden with Christ in God. When Christ who is our life appears, then you also will appear with Him in glory. Therefore put to death your members which are on the earth: fornication, uncleanness, passion, evil desire, and covetousness, which is idolatry.*

Our focus, as that passage shows, is to be on spiritual things. Our text in Rom. 12 shows that also. How important is your business, your home, your investments, your soul? Jesus put it in perspective in Matt. 16:24-26,

> *Then Jesus said to His disciples, "If anyone desires to come after Me, let him deny himself, and take up his cross, and follow Me. For whoever desires to save his life will lose it, but whoever loses his life for My sake will find it. For what profit is it to a man if he gains the whole world, and loses his own soul? Or what will a man give in exchange for his soul?"*

Listen to how the attitude of the Christian is expressed by Paul. 2 Corinthians 4:16-18,

> *Therefore we do not lose heart. Even though our outward man is perishing, yet the inward man is being renewed day by day. For our light affliction, which is but for a moment, is working for us a far more exceeding and eternal weight of glory, while we do not look at the things which are seen, but at the things which are not seen.*

Instead of conforming to the world, we are to *"walk by faith, not by sight"* because we have become *"new creatures in Christ"* (2 Cor. 5:7, 17). Our goal, focus, and hope are different from that of the world.

Don't Let the World Set the Standard

Too many people are wearing the name of Christ while forming a coalition with the practices of the world. Some have become so conditioned by worldly standards, that sin is not only condoned but sanctioned and joined. The line of demarcation between the world and Christ has become obliterated by such conduct. After naming various kinds of "works of the flesh," the apostle Paul then warns in Galatians 5:19-21,

> *Those who practice such things will not inherit the kingdom of God.*

There is a lot of "peer pressure" with which we have to contend, at every stage of life. Teens often say, as they try to persuade their parents to give them permission for some questionable activity, "Everyone is doing it." Young adults and older adults face exactly the same peer pressure. Of course, the truth is, not everyone is doing it. And even if they were, we still dare not let the world set the standard of morality by which we live. If we continue to allow Hollywood, TV, and politicians to set the moral standards of conduct, our society will simply "proceed further in ungodliness". We are called to a higher and better moral standard than the world offers.

The world offers the allure of fame, fortune, and popularity. Christ offers humility, meekness, and service. Instead of avidly seeking after material gain, the Christian follows the injunction of the Lord:

Seek ye first the kingdom of God, and his righteousness, and all these things will be added to you (Matt. 6:33).

There are more important things than bank accounts and big houses. The rich man of Luke 12:15-21 found that out—too late!

The Transformation the Lord Expects

In becoming a Christian, one is *"born of water and the Spirit"* (John 3:5), thus being *"baptized into Christ"* (Rom. 6:3-4) and being made a *"child of God"* in Christ (Gal. 3:26-27). That means that a new life is expected:

Therefore, if anyone is in Christ, he is a new creation; old things have passed away; behold, all things have become new (2 Cor. 5:17).

This new life in Christ calls for a different direction and different emphasis than the world has:

That you put off, concerning your former conduct, the old man ... that you put on the new man which was created according to God, in true righteousness and holiness (Eph. 4:22, 24).

This adjustment is not easy, but with God's help, we can make it.

Once we set our affections on *"things above, where Christ is"* (Col. 3:2), we will not yearn so much to conform to this world. God's people ought to turn in disgust from the sexual immoralities, the lying, moral filth, crime and such. Rather than adjusting to, or conforming to, this world in these matters, we need to show by our lives a higher standard, the standard of morality which God has taught us in His word.

Some say, "We have a lot to learn from the world about how to influence people." Maybe this is true. But it doesn't help to make progress if we are heading in the wrong direction! The great need of the church today is not for better adjustment to the world, and conforming to its methods. It is for all of us to live the life of Christ before the world. We must set our affections on "things above" and show to the world that we are more interested in being "transformed" into the image of Christ than in being conformed to the world.

Dangers in the Church Today (Part One)

From many sources, and in many different forms of writing, we hear dire predictions about the church today, because of the dangers we face. Well, we do face dangers, very serious ones. That is not really anything new. In every age since that Pentecost when the church began (Acts 2), there have been dangers to the church. The apostles of the Lord, in the Scriptures, warned us repeatedly about such dangers. Paul warned elders,

> *From among yourselves men will rise up, speaking perverse things, to draw away the disciples after themselves (Acts 20:28-30).*

Again, writing to a young preacher, Paul wrote,

> *For the time will come when they will not endure sound doctrine, but according to their own desires, because they have itching ears, they will heap up for themselves teachers; and they will turn their ears away from the truth, and be turned aside to fables (2 Tim. 4:3-4).*

Jesus also warned,

> *Beware of false prophets, who come to you in sheep's clothing, but inwardly they are ravenous wolves (Matt 7:15).*

But more than from false teachers who lead Christians astray, there are dangers from within ourselves:

> *Beware, brethren, lest there be in any of you an evil heart of unbelief in departing from the living God (Heb. 3:12).*

> *Each one is tempted when he is drawn away by his own desires and enticed. Then, when desire has conceived, it gives birth to sin; and sin, when it is full-grown, brings forth death (James 1:14-15).*

> *Do not love the world or the things in the world. If anyone loves the world, the love of the Father is not in him. For all that is in the world—the lust of the flesh, the lust of the eyes, and the pride of life—is not of the Father but is of the world (1 John 2:15-16).*

Today, and next week, we are going to look at some of the dangers which threaten the church of the Lord today.

The Danger of Materialism

We live in a materialistic society. Success is measured in riches instead of righteousness, in what we have instead of what we are, in what we own instead of what we do. Instead of loving people and using things, we have reversed that to loving things and using people. In our search for security, we have largely forgotten the need for the Savior. The media, commenting on the morals of this country, have boasted in the past that the morality of our country's leaders is not important, as long as the economy is good.

We need to re-focus, and set the pattern for others to do the same:

One's life does not consist in the abundance of the things he possesses (Luke 12:15).

Jesus followed those words with the story of the rich man who trusted in his riches to provide all he needed. This man would *"pull down his barns, and build greater"* (v. 18).

But God said to him, "Fool! This night your soul will be required of you; then whose will those things be which you have provided?" So is he who lays up treasure for himself, and is not rich toward God (v. 20).

In a similar way, the apostle Paul taught about the dangers of trusting in material things:

Now godliness with contentment is great gain. For we brought nothing into this world, and it is certain we can carry nothing out. And having food and clothing, with these we shall be content. But those who desire to be rich fall into temptation and a snare, and into many foolish and harmful lusts which drown men in destruction and perdition. For the love of money is a root of all kinds of evil, for which some have strayed from the faith in their greediness, and pierced themselves through with many sorrows (1 Tim 6:6-10).

It isn't wrong to have possessions, but we must properly use them. The Lord admonishes,

Command those who are rich in this present age not to be haughty, nor to trust in uncertain riches but in the living God, who gives us richly all things to enjoy. Let them do good, that they be rich in good works, ready to give, willing to share, storing up for themselves a good foundation for the time to come, that they may lay hold on eternal life (1 Tim 6:17-19).

We must "love our neighbor" if we would serve Jesus, and that means being willing to use our resources to help those who need our help.

Danger of Non-Involvement

"No one wants to get involved," said the police captain on the television news, as he reported how a victim had been beaten to death in the presence of dozens of people who made no effort to stop the killers. If you watch the news, you know that has happened many times over the past few years. The one who tries to help is the exception, not the rule. And this same kind of attitude has crept into the Lord's church. Members want to be served, but many are just not interested in serving the church nor are they interested in serving other people.

Jesus said,

So likewise, whoever of you does not forsake all that he has cannot be My disciple (Luke 14:33).

One of the greatest needs in the church today is members who will commit to the Lord and His church—with all that they have and all that they are. Jesus exhorts us to *"Seek first the kingdom of God, and His righteousness"* (Matt. 6:33). When members of the body of Christ expect the "minister" and the elders to visit the sick, teach the lost, and tend to the needy, we are in real trouble. That is the work of all the members! There is no such thing as a "proxy" religion, in which someone else does your service for you. *"So then each of us shall give account of himself to God"* (Rom. 14:12).

We are in danger of forgetting an elementary principle: We are the church! If the church feeds the hungry, members must do it (Acts 11:29-30). If the church restores the erring, members must do it (Gal. 6:1-2). If the church teaches the lost, the members must do it (Matt. 28:19-20). If the church edifies and strengthens the disciples, the members must do it (Acts 9:31). In fact, there is nothing the church can do, unless the members act. Thus, the strength of the church of Jesus Christ on earth is determined by the faith and works of the members of His church. If we don't all get involved, the church can do nothing.

The Danger of Ignorance

God constantly warned Israel, under the Old Testament, that they must learn and teach His will.

> *Beware, lest you forget the Lord who brought you out of the land of Egypt, from the house of bondage ... You shall diligently keep the commandments of the Lord your God, His testimonies, and His statutes which He has commanded you" (Deut. 6:12, 17).*

But Israel too often forgot,

> *Can a virgin forget her ornaments, or a bride her attire? Yet my people have forgotten Me days without number (Jer. 2:32).*

In a generation that has some knowledge of religion but very little knowledge of what the Bible actually says, the Lord's church is in danger of becoming just like the denominational world. We have folks in the church today who speak of "my pastor" and "what our church believes." Many have no basic understanding of the authority of the word of God, and thus are ready to accept the denominational concepts with regard to the worship of the church, or even its basic organization. However, on the other end of the spectrum, in order to separate ourselves from every appearance of the denominational world, we have neglected areas of involvement and fellowship which are completely biblical.

Jesus tells us plainly, *"You shall know the truth, and the truth shall make you free"* (John 8:32). Our salvation is *"through the knowledge of Him who called us"* (2 Pet. 1:3). There is just no substitute for knowledge of the word of God. The people of Berea were commended for their attitude toward the word of God, and their response to that word:

> *These were more fair-minded than those in Thessalonica, in that they received the word with all readiness, and searched the Scriptures daily (Acts 17:11).*

Unless we love the word of God enough to study it diligently, we will never know how to please God. No one can live better than he has learned how to live.

Jesus pointed out,

He who rejects Me, and does not receive My words, has that which judges him—the word that I have spoken will judge him in the last day (John 12:48).

If we are to be judged by that word, we had better learn what is in it! That is one reason the Lord tells us,

Contend earnestly for the faith, which was once for all delivered to the saints (Jude 3).

And, just as Israel was told to teach their children, from the cradle up (Deut. 6:7), so must we.

And the things that you have heard from me among many witnesses, commit these to faithful men who will be able to teach others also (2 Tim. 2:2).

If we are to avoid the dangers of ignorance, we must both learn and teach the word of the Lord.

The Danger of Immorality

The apostle Paul wrote of the ungodliness of the Gentiles, in turning away from God.

Therefore God also gave them up to uncleanness, in the lusts of their hearts, to dishonor their bodies among themselves, who exchanged the truth of God for the lie, and worshiped and served the creature rather than the Creator, who is blessed forever. Amen.

For this reason God gave them up to vile passions. For even their women exchanged the natural use for what is against nature. Likewise also the men, leaving the natural use of the woman, burned in their lust for one another, men with men committing what is shameful, and receiving in themselves the penalty of their error which was due.

And even as they did not like to retain God in their knowledge, God gave them over to a debased mind, to do those things which are not fitting; being filled with all unrighteousness, sexual immorality, wickedness, covetousness, maliciousness; full of envy, murder, strife, deceit, evil-mindedness; they are whisperers, backbiters, haters of God, violent, proud, boasters, inventors of evil things, disobedient to parents (Rom 1:24-30).

That sounds very much like our society today, doesn't it? People engaging in adultery, lying, homosexual activity, murder, etc., and then that society defending their "right" to act that way!

The *"works of the flesh"* (Gal. 5:19-21) are still prevalent today. But God warned,

Woe to those who call evil good, and good evil; who put darkness for light, and light for darkness; who put bitter for sweet, and sweet for bitter! (Isa 5:20).

The evils of drunkenness, some modern dancing, divorce, and the dirt of illicit sex plague our world, and are commonly recognized as acceptable behavior. And these things are becoming more and more common in the church.

My brethren, these things ought not so to be (James 3:10).

The Lord's people must live by a higher standard than that of the world! The Lord commands us,

Love not the world (1 John 2:15).

If you were of the world, the world would love its own: but because you are not of the world, but I chose you out of the world, therefore the world hates you" (John 15:19).

Members of the church of the Lord must not allow the world to set the standards of morality by which we live. We must rise to a higher standard of morality—that revealed in God's word.

The dangers mentioned this morning are mostly from within the church—that is, from within ourselves. They begin in our hearts (James 1:13-15). In Part 2 we will look at four more dangers in the church today. These dangers sometimes come from outside influences, but infect members of the body of Christ just as a disease infects the human body. We will discuss sectarianism, liberalism, Phariseeism, and forgetting our real purpose in the world.

Dangers in the Church Today
(Part Two)

In last week's lesson we looked at four grave dangers in the Lord's church today. These dangers were:

1. **Materialism** – the danger of affluence causing us to "*be at ease in Zion*" (Amos 6:1), trusting in our possessions for security instead of "*seeking first the kingdom of God*" (Matt. 6:33).
2. **Non-Involvement** – the danger that members of the Lord's church will wait for others to do the work of the Lord, instead of becoming actively involved.
3. **Ignorance** – the danger that we will lose our identity as a Bible-loving, Bible-studying, and Bible-quoting people. It is still the truth of God's word that makes us free (John 8:32; 17:17).
4. **Immorality** – the danger that we will allow the world to establish the standard of morality. We must not *be conformed to this world, but be transformed* (Rom. 12:2).

In part two this morning, we are going to discuss four more dangers in the church today.

The Danger of Sectarianism

We need to keep always in our minds and hearts the value of the church of the Lord. Jesus said, "*I will build my church*" (Matt. 16:18). The Lord, by the preaching of the apostles, built that church (Acts 2). And He never built another, nor did He ever authorize anyone to become a member of any other church. Look at the value He placed on that church:

The church of God which he purchased with His own blood (Acts 20:28)

Christ is head of the church; and He is the Savior of the body... and gave Himself for her (Eph. 5:23,25).

That church is His kingdom (Matt. 16:18-19), His body (Col. 1:18), His bride (Eph. 5:22-32), the family of God (1 Tim. 3:15).

The religious world readily accepts the idea of "diversity" of faiths, churches, and other religious areas. But it is really strange to me to see these ideas creeping into the church which Jesus built. Look at the prayer of Jesus:

I do not pray for these [the apostles] alone, but also for those who will believe in Me through their word; that they all may be one, as You, Father, are in Me, and I in You; that they also may be one in Us, that the world may believe that You sent Me (John 17:20-21).

Again, the Lord commanded through Paul,

Now I plead with you, brethren, by the name of our Lord Jesus Christ, that you all speak the same thing, and that there be no divisions among you ... Is Christ divided? (1 Cor. 1:10-13).

The Scripture exhorts,

Keep the unity of the Spirit in the bond of peace (Eph, 4:3).

Then follows,

There is one body and one Spirit, just as you were called in one hope of your calling; one Lord, one faith, one baptism; one God and Father of all, who is above all, and through all, and in you all (Eph. 4:4-6).

We can no more accept, endorse or fellowship the idea of many churches than we can the idea of many gods! Just as there is "one Lord" (Christ), there is "one body" (the church of Christ, Col. 1:18).

We have some in the church today (even in the pulpits!) who speak of the Lord's church as though it were just one denomination among many. If the church of Christ is a denomination, it has no more right to exist than any other man-made institution! According to the word of God, anything different than the church we read about in the NT is not pleasing to the Lord. He prayed, and commanded, that there never be any denomination (any division) at all.

And, with regard to the "other churches," Scripture demands:

Come out from among them, and be separate (2 Cor. 6:17)

And have no fellowship with the unfruitful works of darkness, but rather expose them (Eph. 5:11).

The Lord has called us *out* of false religions. So let us not seek to be entangled in them again.

The Danger of Liberalism

The word "liberalism" means: "Advocating a broad interpretation of the Bible, freedom from rigid doctrine and authoritarianism" (Webster). For many years, religious leaders have sought to nullify the authority of the Bible. They will sometimes make the claim that the Bible is not really the word of God, but that it contains mostly the ideas of men about the nature of God. It is not surprising that these same ideas are now filtering into the church which Jesus built. But we must find our identity as the true church of Christ by acknowledging the Bible as our only authority in all religious matters.

Paul wrote, showing how the Scriptures came to us,

All Scripture is given by inspiration of God, and is profitable for doctrine, for reproof, for correction, for instruction in righteousness, that the man of God may be complete, thoroughly equipped for every good work (2 Tim. 3:16-17).

The apostle Peter said:

Knowing this first, that no prophecy of Scripture is of any private interpretation, for prophecy never came by the will of man, but holy men of God spoke as they were moved by the Holy Spirit (2 Pet. 1:20-21).

Modern preachers may question the source and authority of the Scriptures, but Peter and Paul sure didn't! That is why Paul wrote,

> *When you received the word of God which you heard from us, you welcomed it not as the word of men, but as it is in truth, the word of God, which also effectively works in you who believe (1 Thes. 2:13).*

Jesus said, "*All authority has been given to me*" (Matt. 28:18). He reminds us that His word will judge us in the last day (John 12:48). We are not going to be judged by what some preacher tells us the Bible means—we will be judged by what the word of the Lord actually says. That is why it is so important, in all that we do, that we "Speak where the Bible speaks, and are silent where the Bible is silent." We must know the word of the Lord. But we also must accept that word as our authority for all that we do in religion. In other words—with regard to any worship activity—if Jesus, "*head of the body, the church*" (Col. 1:18), is not the author of it, there is no authority for it!

The Danger of Phariseeism

The Pharisees with whom Jesus dealt during His ministry made many mistakes, and it seems that some today want to repeat them. The Pharisees "knew" that they "had the truth," and as a result, anyone who disagreed with them was a false teacher:

> *Also He spoke this parable to some who trusted in themselves that they were righteous, and despised others (Luke 18:9).*

The Pharisees knew the Scriptures, as their discussions with Jesus showed. They read it, studied it, taught it and debated it. But they often had trouble forming their attitudes by it.

The Pharisees demanded the right to impose their understanding upon others. A good example is the event which is recorded in Matt. 15:6-9 and Mark 7:5-9. Jesus and His disciples ate without first washing their hands. The Jews had a rule that everyone must first wash his hands before eating. They reasoned that washing hands before eating was good, and therefore everybody should do it. If one wanted to be right with God he would wash his hands before eating.

But when those Jewish leaders tried to impose that understanding on Jesus and His disciples, the Lord said,

> *You have made the commandment of God of no effect by your tradition ... In vain they worship Me, teaching as doctrines the commandments of men (Matt. 15:6-9).*

What the Pharisees missed is still being missed by some preachers and many members in the church today. That is the fact that God intends each of us to study the Bible for himself. He never appointed any man, nor group of men, to act as interpreters of the Bible. Each Christian must study and develop his own faith and understanding.

Few of us have difficulty with what the Bible says. It is really rather easy to read. The trouble often comes when we try to apply its teaching to a given situation – especially in the lives of other people! The Pharisees of Jesus' day "explained" what God's word meant, and demanded that others accept that explanation. These religious leaders were the "brotherhood regulators" of their day. But they made a mistake that some are repeating today. They assumed that they were right in their understanding of what God meant, then they forced their "understanding" on other people.

But here is the problem. If God wasn't able to say what He meant so that we could understand it, how in the world can a mere man explain it so that we can understand it? The fact is, when the

Pharisees imposed their "understanding" on others, they were really imposing their traditions and making law of them (Matt. 15; Mark 7). The same principle is at work today. That attitude leaves no room for Christian liberty (Romans 14). And remember this: When we stand before God, we will be judged by what Jesus said, not by what someone tells us that God meant to say or should have said!

Danger of Forgetting Our Purpose

Jesus tells us,

> *If you were of the world, the world would love its own. Yet because you are not of the world, but I chose you out of the world, therefore the world hates you (John 15:19).*

Although we live in the world, we are not to live as the world. Jesus implores,

> *Come out from among them, and be separate (2 Cor. 6:17).*

We often hear people speak of how a certain group, religious or otherwise, "Is far ahead of us" in some area of good work. Well, I've got news for them – they can't be ahead of us, we are not headed in the same direction! The purpose of the Lord's church is distinct and different from every other religious or secular group on earth.

Our purpose is not found in this world. The Lord Jesus has entrusted us with the gospel, which is *"the power of God to salvation"* (Rom. 1:16). Just as Jesus came to *"seek and save the lost"*, so the church has that as her mission in this world. The Lord said,

> *Go into all the world and preach the gospel to every creature. He who believes and is baptized will be saved; but he who does not believe will be condemned (Mark 16:15-16).*

The early disciples took that seriously. Beginning in Jerusalem, *"They did not cease teaching and preaching Jesus as the Christ"* (Acts 5:42). When persecution drove them out of that city, they *"went everywhere preaching the word"* (Acts 8:4). Those early Christians felt this responsibility so keenly that Paul wrote later,

> *Since we have the same spirit of faith, according to what is written, "I believed and therefore I spoke," we also believe and therefore speak (2 Cor. 4:13).*

Many religious groups get involved in politics, or "human rights" issues, or social improvements. But the mission of the church which Jesus built is spiritual in nature. While it is good to feed the hungry (in fact, we *must* feed the hungry), we must recognize that to feed the body while the soul starves is absolute failure of our mission. Jesus said, *"My kingdom is not of this world"* (John 18:36). What we offer to the world is unique. Christ came to save sinners, and none can be saved without Him. We must never forget that Jesus said, *"You have the poor with you always, but Me you do not have always"* (Matt. 26:11). We must remember that our mission is to bring the lost to Jesus Christ. Let's never get sidetracked from that.

Yes, there are dangers in the church today. And these can lead the church astray and make it just another denominational group. But there have been dangers in every generation, and there will continue to be. Let us keep our focus on Christ as the only Savior, on His church as the only body, and His word as the only authority. Then let us make up our minds to remain true to the charge which the Lord gives us as His body, the church He built and bought with His blood. Let us stand and sing.

Despised and Rejected of Men

Look at Isaiah 53:3-5,

> *He is despised and rejected by men, a Man of sorrows and acquainted with grief. And we hid, as it were, our faces from Him; He was despised, and we did not esteem Him. Surely He has borne our griefs and carried our sorrows; yet we esteemed Him stricken, smitten by God, and afflicted. But He was wounded for our transgressions, He was bruised for our iniquities; the chastisement for our peace was upon Him, and by His stripes we are healed.*

This prophecy points out the shameful manner in which the Son of God, Israel's Messiah, the Christ, would be rebuffed and rejected of men when He should come to save them. No Scripture, from either the Old Testament or New, more graphically discloses the shameful way in which He was despised and rejected. When you have time go back and read the entire 53rd chapter of Isaiah.

John said of Christ,

> *He came to His own, and His own did not receive Him. But as many as received Him, to them He gave the right to become children of God, to those who believe in His name (John 1:11-12).*

Even though eternal life was freely offered to them, they *"did not receive Him."* And in rejecting Him, they were also rejecting God who had sent Him. Jesus said,

> *He who does not honor the Son does not honor the Father who sent Him (John 5:23).*

To this He also added the warning,

> *He who rejects Me, and does not receive My words, has that which judges him—the word that I have spoken will judge him in the last day (John 12:48).*

How fearful it is to reject and despise the Son of God, and yet so many folks do so, even today. In spite of their proclamations that they believe in Him, Jesus Christ is still *"despised and rejected of men, a man of sorrows and acquainted with grief!"*

Some Reject the Divinity of Jesus

In making the promise to Mary, the angel of the Lord said,

> *That Holy One who is to be born will be called the Son of God. (Luke 1:35).*

The angel of the Lord also appeared unto Joseph with the promise,

> *And she will bring forth a Son, and you shall call His name Jesus, for He will save His people from their sins.*

And he further stated that the name would be Immanuel, which means *"God with us"* (Matt. 1:21-23). After Jesus was baptized of John, the voice of God proclaimed,

> *You are My beloved Son; in You I am well pleased (Luke 3:22).*

In speaking to Nicodemus, Jesus said,

> *For God so loved the world that He gave His only begotten Son, that whoever believes in Him should not perish but have everlasting life (John 3:16).*

And yet again in John 5:22, Jesus claimed to be the Son of God.

When the claims of Jesus of Nazareth are set against the background of His miracles and wonders performed to confirm and establish those claims, it becomes increasingly difficult to understand how the House of Israel could then reject their long-awaited Messiah. It is no less difficult to understand how intelligent, rational people can still reject and despise the loving Savior of men! But it seems there has never been a time when the Son of God has been despised and rejected by so many. Modernists and infidels are more and more openly rejecting the Christ. It brings to mind the words of 1 John 2:22,

> *Who is a liar but he who denies that Jesus is the Christ? He is antichrist who denies the Father and the Son.*

Their vain attempts to humanize God and deify the reasoning of man have led them into efforts that strip Christ of His divinity.

It was prophesied that these things should come to pass.

> *But there were also false prophets among the people, even as there will be false teachers among you, who will secretly bring in destructive heresies, even denying the Lord who bought them, and bring on themselves swift destruction. And many will follow their destructive ways, because of whom the way of truth will be blasphemed (2 Pet. 2:1-2).*

The child of God cannot afford to have any dealings with these false teachers.

> *For many deceivers have gone out into the world who do not confess Jesus Christ as coming in the flesh... Whoever transgressesand does not abide in the doctrine of Christ does not have God. He who abides in the doctrine of Christ has both the Father and the Son. If anyone comes to you and does not bring this doctrine, do not receive him into your house nor greet him; for he who greets him shares in his evil deeds (2 John 7-11).*

In this same way, today, Jesus Christ is "despised and rejected of men."

Many Reject the Authority of Christ

While He was still on earth, just before His ascension, Jesus said, "*All authority has been given to Me in heaven and on earth*" (Matt 28:18). Again He said,

> *For as the Father has life in Himself, so He has granted the Son to have life in Himself, and has given Him authority to execute judgment also, because He is the Son of Man (John 5:26-27).*

Further concerning that authority, the Lord stated,

He who rejects Me, and does not receive My words, has that which judges him—the word that I have spoken will judge him in the last day (John 12:48).

Unfortunately that great authority is rejected and despised by multitudes today. Though the Holy Spirit has declared that Jesus Christ is *"the blessed and only Potentate, the King of kings and Lord of lords, who alone has immortality"* (1 Tim. 6:15-16), many still would set up councils, synods, and conferences to eclipse His authority and take from His grandeur! These bring forth abridgments and revisions of His gospel, as though they had legislative authority!

Paul declared,

I marvel that you are turning away so soon from Him who called you in the grace of Christ, to a different gospel, which is not another; but there are some who trouble you and want to pervert the gospel of Christ. But even if we, or an angel from heaven, preach any other gospel to you than what we have preached to you, let him be accursed (Gal. 1:6-8).

Still, it cannot be denied that there are many gospels being preached which Paul did not proclaim. In Acts 20:29-30, Paul said,

For I know this, that after my departure savage wolves will come in among you, not sparing the flock. Also from among yourselves men will rise up, speaking perverse things, to draw away the disciples after themselves.

Paul foretold that some would despise and reject the authority of Jesus Christ.

Human Doctrines Reject Christ's Doctrines

As Jesus was leaving His disciples, He charged them to go into all the world and preach the gospel to every creature (see Matt. 28:18-20; Mark 16:15-16; Luke 24:46-49). This message meant salvation to all who would accept it, for it was God's power to save. But it was not long before this saving message had become contaminated, being perverted by unholy men (see Gal. 1:6-8). Even while our Lord was on earth, He confronted some who were not willing to abide in God's teachings:

These people draw near to Me with their mouth, and honor Me with their lips, but their heart is far from Me. And in vain they worship Me, teaching as doctrines the commandments of men (Matt. 15:8-9).

Later Paul gave a warning,

Now the Spirit expressly says that in latter times some will depart from the faith, giving heed to deceiving spirits (1 Tim. 4:1).

The apostle to the Gentiles then disclosed the manner of this departure, so that we might be both forewarned and fore-armed.

In current religious circles, one may find almost any idea being set forth for binding faith and practice. The creed books which men have foisted on the ignorant and unlearned are accepted with devotion and fidelity. Without questioning where they have come from, Catechisms, Prayer

Books, Disciplines, Manuals, Articles of Faith, and such church books have been voluntarily accepted as binding. After having aligned themselves with religious groups unknown by inspired men, individuals wearing names unheard of in the Bible have accepted guidance from sources "not from heaven, but of men." They have despised and rejected the Christ, by refusing His gospel which could save them! And against all these, the host of plagues await (see Rev. 22:18-19).

Many People Reject the Worship Christ Ordained

The worship which Jesus Christ ordained has also been despised and rejected! In John 4:24, Jesus said,

God is a Spirit: and they that worship Him must worship Him in spirit and in truth.

The items of New Testament worship have been too plainly presented to be overlooked or discounted. From such verses as Acts 2:42; Col. 3:16; 1 Cor. 11:23-26; 1 Cor. 16:1-2; Acts 20:7 and others, we find there were public prayers, the reading and preaching of God's Word, singing, making melody in the heart to the Lord, giving of their means, and the remembrance of the Lord's death, burial, and resurrection in the Lord's Supper. The simplicity of this order of worship allows no misunderstanding. It was free from stratagems or vain formality. However, even while Jesus was in His personal ministry, He had to rebuke some for their pretense in prayers and hypocritical show of worship (see Matt 23:14-33).

Paul had learned this lesson well, and wrote,

What is it then? I will pray with the spirit, and I will pray with the understanding also: I will sing with the spirit, and I will sing with the understanding, also (1 Cor. 14:15).

It would be utterly impossible to give exact figures on the number who present a form of worship during religious services whose hearts are far from God.

It is a great task to worship in spirit and in truth. It is easy to let the mind wander, and allow carnal thoughts to crowd out devotion! To follow this path of least resistance means that we have despised and rejected the worship Jesus Christ has ordained for our own! And thereby we, too, may despise and reject the Christ!

Time would fail me if I should try to list for you all the ways in which the worship ordained by the Lord has been despised by the introductions of innovations! But be sure to take note, each innovation stands as a monument to people who despised the true worship Jesus Christ set forth! Each innovation dishonors Christ! It shows that we despise and reject His way for our own! And because of the selfishness of men, Jesus is still "despised and rejected of men."

Brothers and sisters don't be caught despising and rejecting Christ. Christ is divine. Christ is the authority of man. The standard set for us to follow is the word of God. The worship we must participate in is that put forth in Scripture.

Can We Really Live For Jesus?

There are those who teach that it is not possible for human beings to live up to the standard of godliness that Christianity demands. The devil would like for us to accept that heresy to discourage us from even trying to live for God. Do we have certain propensities within us that prohibit a closer walk with God? Did our Creator make us with an inbuilt spiritual deficiency that makes it certain that we will fail in our pursuit of holiness? Or, are there helps along the way that enable us to glorify the Savior? In the language of Rom. 4:3 I ask: *"What do the Scriptures say?"*

In the beauty of Psa. 119:76-80, we find some wonderful sources of consolation and joy:

> *Let, I pray, Your merciful kindness be for my comfort, according to Your word to Your servant. Let Your tender mercies come to me, that I may live; for Your law is my delight. Let the proud be ashamed, for they treated me wrongfully with falsehood; but I will meditate on Your precepts. Let those who fear You turn to me, those who know Your testimonies. Let my heart be blameless regarding Your statutes, that I may not be ashamed.*

From this we take comfort in the following:
1. God's judgments are right
2. God's merciful kindness comforts
3. God's law is my delight
4. God's precepts are my meditation
5. My heart is blameless regarding His statutes.

Jesus taught,

> *But seek first the kingdom of God and His righteousness, and all these things shall be added to you (Matt. 6:33).*

Do you know why most of the world is lost? It hinges on Matt. 6:33. Instead of seeking first the kingdom of God, the vast majority of people all over the world are seeking food, clothing, and shelter first and putting God last. Jesus challenges us and gives us the best insurance policy ever issued, now or to the end of time, in Matt. 6:33. Not many people take the Lord seriously on that promise. It is a tragedy how that high ethical standard is ignored!

We Have the Promise of Help from Heaven

It is challenging to live a life of purity and spiritual integrity, but we get substantial help from the God of heaven. When we live such a life we receive many benefits and blessings: God's promises, provisions, protection, providence, power, prayer, and propitiation. Once these matters are explored in the sacred text, we can fully see that God has not asked us to do the impossible, but rather enables us to follow in the footprints of our Redeemer! So let's take a look at them.

Promises

The wonderful promises of the gospel age surround us. Peter writes,

Grace and peace be multiplied to you in the knowledge of God and of Jesus our Lord, as His divine power has given to us all things that pertain to life and godliness, through the knowledge of Him who called us by glory and virtue (2 Pet. 1:2-3).

These promises encourage us to know that the Lord will never forsake us and will bless us with all spiritual blessings in Christ, as long as we continue to walk with him.

Provisions

When our lives are lives of purity and spiritual integrity, the Lord will provide us with all of our needs. James wrote,

Every good gift and every perfect gift is from above, and comes down from the Father of lights (James 1:17)

And the apostle Paul added,

And my God shall supply all your need according to His riches in glory by Christ Jesus (Phil. 4:19).

Protection

When we walk with God, we can look for and expect constant protection from above as long as the world stands:

Lo, I am with you always, even to the end of the age (Matt. 28:20).

He will be with us in all situations and provide avenues of escape, regardless of severe trials and the chicanery of the devil.

No temptation has overtaken you except such as is common to man; but God is faithful, who will not allow you to be tempted beyond what you are able, but with the temptation will also make the way of escape, that you may be able to bear it (1 Cor. 10:13).

The psalmist wrote,

Our help is in the name of the Lord, Who made heaven and earth (Psa. 124:8).

Providence

Those who live a life of spiritual purity and integrity are in the hands of the One who is able to deliver us (Dan. 3:17). While we are upheld by His arms, no harm can befall us:

The eternal God is your refuge, and underneath are the everlasting arms; He will thrust out the enemy from before you (Deut. 33:27).

Under His wings, we are kept safe:

Keep me as the apple of your eye; hide me under the shadow of Your wings (Psa. 17:8).

In the constant care of God, we are continually sustained and granted peace and spiritual success. We are caused to soar as eagles, regardless of earthly problems and human failures:

> *But those who wait on the Lord shall renew their strength; they shall mount up with wings like eagles, they shall run and not be weary, they shall walk and not faint (Isa. 40:31).*

Power

The power of God motivates us to holiness and sanctity that gets the attention of an unbelieving world. In Acts 4:13 we read of the reaction of unbelievers to the lives of the apostles:

> *Now when they saw the boldness of Peter and John, and perceived that they were uneducated and untrained men, they marveled. And they realized that they had been with Jesus.*

And the apostle Peter caps it all when he writes that we have:

> *...an inheritance incorruptible and undefiled and that does not fade away, reserved in heaven for you, who are kept by the power of God through faith for salvation ready to be revealed in the last time (1 Pet. 1:4-5).*

Prayer

The tremendous concourse of prayer keeps us close to the throne of God and gives us confidence. The Scriptures say,

> *Now this is the confidence that we have in Him, that if we ask anything according to His will, He hears us (1 John 5:14).*

We understand that the door of heaven is always open to us when we ask according to the will of God:

> *Ask, and it will be given to you; seek, and you will find; knock, and it will be opened to you (Matt. 7:7).*

Propitiation

The propitiation of the blood of Jesus Christ has the efficacy to cleanse us and to draw us near to the great reservoir of strength that motivates and cheers us on to higher ground.

> *My little children, these things I write to you, so that you may not sin. And if anyone sins, we have an Advocate with the Father, Jesus Christ the righteous. And He Himself is the propitiation for our sins, and not for ours only but also for the whole world (1 John 2:1-2).*

Those who teach that it is not possible for people to live up to the standard of godliness that Christianity demands are wrong. Yes, we can live the life the Bible sets forth because we get so much help from the Savior. May we never turn back.

The Power of a Life of Purity

Christianity demands our very best because it is demonstrated by purity of life. The basic, fundamental values of the religion of Christ can best be seen in His life:

For we do not have a High Priest who cannot sympathize with our weaknesses, but was in all points tempted as we are, yet without sin (Heb. 4:15).

Him who knew no sin [became] sin for us, that we might become the righteousness of God in Him (2 Cor. 5:21).

It was said of Jesus, "*He went about doing good*" (Acts 10:38). So do His followers, because Christ "*suffered for us, leaving us an example, that you should follow His steps*" (1 Pet. 2:21). The same values seen in the life of Jesus are seen in the dedicated demeanor of His fervent disciples.

Too many times the world receives a faulty impression of the way of the cross because of our failure to portray the ethics of godliness. In Paul's letter to the Philippians, we learn anew of the intense value and power of a life that magnifies Christ and shares the message of the Redeemer with others,

According to my earnest expectation and hope that in nothing I shall be ashamed, but with all boldness, as always, so now also Christ will be magnified in my body, whether by life or by death. For to me, to live is Christ, and to die is gain (Phil. 1:20-21).

What demands the gospel places upon devotees of the Savior! There is a stanza of a beautiful gospel song that ought to ring in the ears of every Christian:

Let the beauty of Jesus be seen in me,
All His wonderful passion and purity,
May His spirit divine, all my being refine,
Let the beauty of Jesus be seen in me.

The Power of a Living Hope

Christianity is great because it brings hope, optimism, and joy into the daily walk of children of the heavenly Father. Trusting in the Creator, instead of earth's vain trinkets, gives us the enrichment that only the hope of heaven can grant to us. Hope includes faith, but it also is assurance. We have that because of the resurrection of Jesus:

God ... has begotten us again to a living hope through the resurrection of Jesus Christ from the dead (1 Pet. 1:3).

Christians, never look back to a life of sin, but ever press on to the beautiful home of the soul. Let us all rise up to meet the challenge of Christianity. With a firm commitment and deep resolve, we will one day, by the grace of God, when the saints go marching into glory, join in that heavenly chorus.

Can I Trust My Bible?

If you go to any bookstore today you will find a large selection of "How To" books. These books will tell you how to have a beautiful flower garden or a bountiful vegetable garden. If you look further you can learn how to cook a low fat dinner, or you can learn how to change the oil in your car. There are books on how to be better spouses and parents. There are "How To" books that teach you about investing, retirement and lots of other things as well.

Mankind *really* needs one "How To" text. This is the book that guides man through life, the one that tells him what his life is about and why he is alive at all. This would be a book that explains suffering and death. There are many efforts made to provide this text. Some philosophies try to tell man how to improve life, either by indulging in pleasure or by denying himself pleasure. Some sciences try to improve life by explaining the mind, its health, and its illnesses. But again, these different sciences disagree on how to accomplish what they all want to accomplish. From philosophy to science to religion there are many sources trying to be the ultimate "How To" book.

One book steps up and makes a startling claim. The Bible claims to be THE "How To" text of all times and for all times. Look with me at 1 Peter 1:22-25.

> *Since you have purified your souls in obeying the truth through the Spirit in sincere love of the brethren, love one another fervently with a pure heart, having been born again, not of corruptible seed but incorruptible, through the word of God which lives and abides forever, because 'all flesh is as grass, and all the glory of man as the flower of the grass. The grass withers, and its flower falls away, but the word of the Lord endures forever.' Now this is the word which by the gospel was preached to you.*

The Bible claims to endure forever, while all of man's efforts and explanations fade and die. Many have opposed the Bible, many have attempted to destroy it, but still it survives and abounds even today. Having lasted for centuries, some might wonder, "Can we trust the Bible?" It is old, parts of it written 1500 years before Christ was born. It is seen as ancient by some and as out of date by many others. Can you trust your Bible?

If You Trust the Historical Evidence

You can trust the Bible if you trust the historical evidence that accompanies it. The Bible was written by 40 different authors over some 1500 to 1600 years. It was written by men of education and political wisdom (as Moses, raised in Pharaoh's house) and by shepherds (like Amos, the prophet). It was written by people who had no place to call home and by people settled in great civilizations. It was written by men who spoke and wrote Hebrew and by men who spoke and wrote Greek.

There is no other book comparable to the Bible in this simple evidence. In spite of the diversity of authors in time, place, and cultures, the Bible is consistent. It teaches a consistent way of life. It presents a God throughout who is the same and unchanging, in spite of the different authors and their different experiences and outlooks. All this indicates a supernatural hand was guiding the compilation of our Bible. Only God could put it all together using so many different sources.

The Bible was written in two commonly spoken languages. The Old Testament was written in common Hebrew, a language still spoken and used today. The common people of ancient times and common people today can still read this ancient language. The New Testament was written in common Greek, the universal language of the era. Yet, in spite of the differences in language and time and place, the entire Old Testament points to the New and the New Testament quotes from and depends on the Old Testament. Again, only the hand of God could guide the making of this book.

Compared to other religions and philosophies, the Bible stands alone. Whereas most religious books and documents are written by one man and usually are all written in one span of time from one cultural perspective, the Bible is not like that. As such, you can trust the Bible since the historical evidence for its compilation is so strong.

If You Trust the Textual Evidence

The Hebrew Old Testament is well proven to be accurate in its text. You would think a book written centuries ago might undergo some serious changes in text due to copying errors and poor transmission of written materials. Yet, when the Dead Sea Scrolls were found, those ancient texts (dating from the first century) matched almost exactly the Hebrew text of our modern Bible. The only alterations were in minor words like "the" or "and." It is remarkable to see how accurate our text is when compared to ancient texts.

The same is true of the Greek New Testament as well. Some of our earliest documents date from the early 200's A.D. Many date from later decades and centuries, but all of our New Testament documents are consistent. There are no major differences in texts from the earliest periods to those of later periods. In both the New and Old Testaments we have ample proof the text has remained unchanged since it was written hundreds of years ago. Again, only the hand of God could insure this sort of accuracy in text.

Compare the Bible to other ancient documents. We have thousands of whole and pieces of the New Testament. They are all the same and consistent in text. We have more evidence for the text of the Bible than for Julius Caesar's life and writings. We have more evidence for the Bible than for the works of Aristotle. In fact, we have much more proof of the Bible's unchanging text than for the works of William Shakespeare! You can trust your Bible since the text has been the same for hundreds and hundreds of years.

If You Trust Its Truths

Ask yourself some simple questions about this "How To" text. Does it make sense? Do its principles work in daily life? Will it make a person happier, healthier, content? These are legitimate questions to ask of a book that claims to endure forever. If it is the best book on how to live, it should offer guidelines that will make life work.

The Bible does every bit of that. It does provide answers on how to be happy, on how to live healthier lives both physically and psychologically. I have heard of therapists who deal with unbelievers. They usually counsel these patients using Biblical principles of life, even though the patient has no idea that was what was happening. Yet, when they applied God's principles (even though ignorant of its source) their lives and relationships always improved. When man applies the Bible's teaching, man's life improves, even if the man doesn't believe. Ghandi was a great leader and a Hindu. But he had read Jesus' teaching on turning the other cheek and going the second mile and became devoted to those principles. Using God's teachings, even though he was not a believer, he was able to overthrow British rule in India. God's book and its teachings make life work. That makes the Bible the best "How To" book ever written.

If You Trust Its Author

Putting your trust in a "How To" book ultimately comes down to what you choose to believe. If there is a God, what does He want from us? Do we make up our own gods, or do we accept the God the Bible reveals? In the final analysis, you must choose. But if you choose to believe in a personal, all powerful God, you can also put your trust in His "How To" book.

Look with me at 2 Peter 1:19-21.

> *And so we have the prophetic word confirmed, which you do well to heed as a light that shines in a dark place, until the day dawns and the morning star rises in your hearts; knowing this first, that no prophecy of Scripture is of any private interpretation, for prophecy never came by the will of man, but holy men of God spoke as they were moved by the Holy Spirit.*

Peter says it simply. God moved men to write. We can trust the Bible because God was behind it, not men. If you trust God, you can trust His Bible.

We all know 2 Timothy 3:16-17, and it is important. Look at it with me.

> *All Scripture is given by inspiration of God, and is profitable for doctrine, for reproof, for correction, for instruction in righteousness, that the man of God may be complete, thoroughly equipped for every good work.*

Paul sums it up best. The Bible is the best "How To" book when it comes to doing good, living right, serving God, raising a family, living and even dying. No other book makes such a claim. No other book backs up its claims with historical, textual, and practical evidence. You can trust your Bible. It is the living, abiding Word of the Living God.

The Bible reveals "How To" become a Christian, and "How To" live as one. If you have not become a Christian or lived like one in a way consistent with Scripture, we would like to help. Let us know about it now, as we stand and sing.

Does God Really Mean It?

I read of someone who was studying a particular passage of the Scripture with a lady, and she had difficulty accepting what God had said. Finally, after she had read the passage several times, she said, "Well I don't think it means that!" The man who was studying with her tried, in vain, to show her that her argument was with God, not him. She didn't just disagree with what he thought the passage meant, she disagreed with what God actually said. As Paul wrote,

> *We also thank God without ceasing, because when you received the word of God which you heard from us, you welcomed it not as the word of men, but as it is in truth, the word of God, which also effectively works in you who believe (1 Thess. 2:13).*

With the emphasis on "political correctness" in our society today, it isn't strange that people do not believe God means what He says. Many seem to feel that God will save them, no matter how they live in this world. If God says, "Do this and you will be blessed," they feel the blessing will be theirs whether they obey Him or not. When Jesus was on trial, He said that He came to bear witness to the truth. Pilate then asked Him, *"What is truth?"* (John 18:38). That rhetorical question implies that there is no absolute truth; or, if there is, we cannot really know it. Our modern society has bought into that same idea. But Jesus knew better. He prayed to the Father, *"Your word is truth"* (John 17:17). So, does God really mean what He says to us today, as revealed in His word, the Scriptures?

Ask Adam and Eve if God Meant It

When God put man in the Garden of Eden, He said:

> *Of every tree of the garden you may freely eat; but of the tree of the knowledge of good and evil you shall not eat, for in the day that you eat of it you shall surely die (Gen 2:16-17).*

Did God really mean it? When Adam and Eve ate of that tree…

> *God said, "Behold, the man has become like one of Us, to know good and evil. And now, lest he put out his hand and take also of the tree of life, and eat, and live forever"— therefore the Lord God sent him out of the garden of Eden to till the ground from which he was taken" (Gen 3:22-23).*

Some will argue, "God is love, and he will forgive, no matter what we do." Well, just ask Adam and Eve if God meant what He said! God always speaks the truth: *"It is impossible for God to lie"* (Heb. 6:18). When God told Adam and Eve not to eat of the tree of knowledge of good and evil, He sure meant what He said! And when He promises to punish us if we disobey, we had better believe that God means it.

Ask Nadab and Abihu if God Meant It

God chose Aaron and his sons to be priests, when He led Israel out of Egypt and gave them the law through Moses. As part of the worship of the tabernacle, the priests were to burn incense, and God was specific about it:

> *Then he shall take a censer full of burning coals of fire from the altar before the Lord (Lev. 16:12).*

I am sure that some today would argue that "fire is fire and it doesn't really matter where they get the fire, if their heart is right." Maybe that is the way those two sons of Aaron thought:

> *Then Nadab and Abihu, the sons of Aaron, each took his censer and put fire in it, put incense on it, and offered profane fire before the Lord, which He had not commanded them. So fire went out from the Lord and devoured them, and they died before the Lord (Lev 10:1-2).*

Just ask Nadab and Abihu if God meant what He said! When God specified the source of the fire to be used to burn the incense, man just didn't have the right to substitute something else. The punishment of Nadab and Abihu may seem a little severe to some people, but what should be the penalty for rebellion against God?! That is exactly what is described in Lev. 10—rebellion. God meant what He said, and He said it plainly.

Ask Uzza If God Meant What He Said

God gave specific instructions about moving the holy things of the sanctuary, including the Ark of Covenant.

> *And when Aaron and his sons have finished covering the sanctuary and all the furnishings of the sanctuary, when the camp is set to go, then the sons of Kohath shall come to carry them; but they shall not touch any holy thing, lest they die (Num. 4:15).*

The ark of covenant was to be carried by staves, which were passed through the rings in either side of the ark, and was to be carried by the "sons of Kohath." Notice what the penalty was for violating what God said: "Lest they die." Did God really mean that?

During the days of King David, the Ark of the Covenant was being transported back to Israel, and God's plan was not followed.

> *Let us bring the ark of our God back to us, for we have not inquired at it since the days of Saul... And when they came to Chidon's threshing floor, Uzza put out his hand to hold the ark, for the oxen stumbled. Then the anger of the Lord was aroused against Uzza, and He struck him because he put his hand to the ark; and he died there before God (1 Chron. 13:3, 9-10).*

Even King David was afraid when He saw what happened to Uzza.

> *David was afraid of God that day, saying, "How can I bring the ark of God to me?" (1 Chron. 13:12).*

The answer was simple—just do what God said! And when David did that, the ark was moved successfully:

> *And David called ... and said to them, "You are the heads of the fathers' houses of the Levites; sanctify yourselves, you and your brethren, that you may bring up the ark of the Lord God of Israel to the place I have prepared for it. For because you did not do it the first time, the Lord our God broke out against us, because we did not consult Him about the proper order." So the priests and the Levites sanctified themselves to bring up the ark of the Lord God of Israel. And the children of the Levites bore the ark of God on their shoulders, by its poles, as Moses had commanded according to the word of the Lord (1 Chron. 15:11-15).*

It should be obvious that God meant what He said about how the ark should be moved!

Ask Naaman if God Meant what He Said

Naaman was a general in the Syrian army, but he was a leper. His wife's servant girl was a captive from Israel, and she told of a prophet there who could heal him. When Naaman finally came to Elisha, the prophet told him that God ordered that he go and dip seven times in the Jordan River and he would be cured of the leprosy. Naaman was angry, and note his response:

> *Are not the Abanah and the Pharpar, the rivers of Damascus, better than all the waters of Israel? Could I not wash in them and be clean?" So he turned and went away in a rage (2 Kings 5:12).*

When he went away in a rage, he was still a leper!
But Naaman's servant sought to persuade him to do what God said:

> *My father, if the prophet had told you to do something great, would you not have done it? How much more then, when he says to you, "Wash, and be clean"? So he went down and dipped seven times in the Jordan, according to the saying of the man of God; and his flesh was restored like the flesh of a little child, and he was clean (2 Kings 5:13-14).*

Naaman was not cleansed because his heart was right, or just because he had enough faith to travel all the way from Damascus to Samaria. He was cleansed of leprosy because he did what God told him. He learned that God meant what He said!

The Lord Still Means What He Says

From the above examples from Old Testament Scriptures, it is clear that:
1. When God says NOT to do something, man cannot do it without being punished.
2. When God says to DO something, man will be punished if he fails to do it.
3. God's promised blessings are predicated upon our doing what He says.

Jesus stated this principle clearly:

Not everyone who says to Me, "Lord, Lord," shall enter the kingdom of heaven, but he who does the will of My Father in heaven (Matt 7:21).

The apostle Paul wrote:

But God be thanked that though you were slaves of sin, yet you obeyed from the heart that form of doctrine to which you were delivered. And having been set free from sin, you became slaves of righteousness (Rom 6:17-18).

The apostle Peter echoed the same theme.

You have purified your souls in obeying the truth (1 Pet. 1:22).

If we would enjoy eternal salvation, we must listen to the Lord.

Though He was a Son, yet He learned obedience by the things which He suffered. And having been perfected, He became the author of eternal salvation to all who obey Him (Heb 5:8-9).

What Must I Do To Be Saved?

The Lord requires faith. When people in the times of the apostles asked, "What must I do to be saved?" what was the Lord's answer? Listen carefully: *"You will die in your sin: where I go, you cannot come ... If you do not believe that I am he, you will die in your sins"* (John 8:21, 24). The inspired Paul and Silas told the Philippian jailer, *"Believe on the Lord Jesus, and you will be saved"* (Acts 16:31). In the great commission, after His death on the cross, Christ told the apostles, *"Go into all the world, and preach the gospel to every creature. He that believes and is baptized will be saved; but he who does not believe shall be condemned"* (Mark 16:15-16). Without faith, *"It is impossible to please God"* (Heb. 11:6).

The Lord requires repentance. Jesus also told the apostles to preach *"Repentance and remission of sins"* (Luke 24:47) to all the world. And they did. On Pentecost, when believers asked what to do, God's answer by the mouth of Peter was, *"Repent, and let every one of you be baptized in the name of Jesus Christ for the remission of sins"* (Acts 2:38). Unless one is willing to turn from His sinful life and live for Jesus, he just cannot be saved. God *"commands all men everywhere to repent"* (Acts 17:30). As the apostle Paul put it, *"How shall we who died to sin live any longer in it?"* (Rom. 6:2).

The Lord also requires baptism. Notice the command and promise of the Lord:

Go into all the world and preach the gospel to every creature. He who believes and is baptized will be saved; but he who does not believe will be condemned (Mark 16:15-16).

This simply explains what the Lord had before told Nicodemus.

Jesus answered, "Most assuredly, I say to you, unless one is born of water and the Spirit, he cannot enter the kingdom of God!" (John 3:5).

When sinners heard the gospel and were "pricked in their heart" on Pentecost (Acts 2:37), and asked what to do, the Lord's reply was:

Repent, and let every one of you be baptized in the name of Jesus Christ for the remission of sins (Acts 2:38).

We all had better approach the Bible with the firm conviction that the Lord really means what He says. We must study carefully Acts 22:16, Rom. 6:3-6, 16-18 and Gal. 3:26-29 and resolve to learn all of the will of God, and do it. We must believe that God means what he says, then act on it. Then we all can have confidence, by His promises, that we will live with Him eternally.

Serve God With All Your Heart

We often hear people speak of "heart-felt" religion, and how important the heart is in our service to God. Moses told the nation of Israel,

Hear, O Israel: The Lord our God, the Lord is one! You shall love the Lord your God with all your heart, with all your soul, and with all your strength (Deut. 6:4-5).

He further exhorted them,

Earnestly obey My commandments which I command you today, to love the Lord your God and serve Him with all your heart and with all your soul (Deut. 11:13).

In a similar vein, the prophet Samuel later preached,

Only fear the Lord, and serve Him in truth with all your heart; for consider what great things He has done for you (1 Sam. 12:24).

We cannot overemphasize the importance of the heart: "*For as he thinks in his heart, so is he*" (Prov. 23:7). The heart determines who we are, and also what we are. But just what is "the heart" of which the Bible speaks? The only way to answer that question is to look to the Scriptures and see what the heart does and how it functions.

The Bible Heart Includes the Intellect

The heart is much more than "feelings." Jesus, when He was confronted with opposition to the good he was doing, asked those objectors, "*Why do you think evil in your hearts?*" (Matt. 9:4). In a similar event, Jesus asked the objectors, "*Why do you reason about these things in your hearts?*" (Mark 2:8). The "heart" of the Bible, then, often means the MIND of man. That part of ourselves that reads and absorbs what is read, then draws conclusions from that reading—that is the heart. The functions of thinking and reasoning are of the heart. Notice again the proverb, "*As he thinks in his heart, so is he.*"

It is with the heart that "understanding" comes, also. Jesus, quoting from Isa. 6, told the Jews:

For the hearts of this people have grown dull. Their ears are hard of hearing, and their eyes they have closed, lest they should see with their eyes and hear with their ears, lest they should understand with their hearts and turn, so that I should heal them" (Matt 13:15).

With the same heart, as we reach an understanding of who Jesus really is, we believe: "*With the heart one believes unto righteousness*" (Rom 10:10). Using the "heart," we hear (or read) the gospel of Jesus Christ. We then, understanding it, believe that Jesus is the Christ, the Son of God. So, "*Faith comes by hearing the word of God*" (Rom. 10:17). To think, to reason, to understand, and to believe are all functions of the intellect—the heart.

The Bible Heart Includes the Emotions

Many people, in thinking of the heart, think only of the emotional part of a person. And it is certainly true that is an important function of what the Bible calls "the heart." For instance, Michal saw David rejoicing over bringing back the Ark of Covenant, *"And she despised him in her heart"* (2 Sam 6:16). Asked about the greatest commandment, Jesus replied,

> *You shall love the Lord your God with all your heart, with all your soul, and with all your mind (Matt 22:37).*

So, the heart despises, and the heart loves. The heart includes the emotions.

Other emotional attributes of the Bible heart are found. The heart "desires" (Rom. 10:1), it "despairs" (Eccl. 2:20), it "rejoices" (Acts 2:26), it "sorrows" (Rom. 9:2; Isa. 65:14). All of these are emotional qualities or reactions. A good example of this function of the heart, and how different emotions are formed, is found in the case of Jacob and his son, Joseph.

The brothers of Joseph, being jealous of him, sold him into slavery. But they took the special coat Jacob had given him and smeared animal blood on it, and then brought it to Jacob. He assumed Joseph had been killed,

> *"It is my son's tunic. A wild beast has devoured him. Without doubt Joseph is torn to pieces." Then Jacob tore his clothes, put sackcloth on his waist, and mourned for his son many days. And all his sons and all his daughters arose to comfort him; but he refused to be comforted (Gen. 37:33-35).*

Years later, when Joseph was found alive, and Jacob had that wonderful reunion with him, his heart rejoiced (Gen. 46). Jacob's heart sorrowed when he thought Joseph was dead, but rejoiced when he learned that he was still alive.

The Bible Heart Includes the Will

The Bible heart makes decisions, determines the course of action to take:

> *Why have you conceived this thing in your heart? (Acts 5:4).*

> *Nevertheless he who stands steadfast in his heart, having no necessity, but has power over his own will, and has so determined in his heart (1 Cor. 7:37).*

Our giving, for instance, is based on the heart:

> *Let each one give as he purposes in his heart (2 Cor. 9:7).*

Not only is our giving based on "purpose of heart," but so is all of man's service to God.

> *Daniel purposed in his heart that he would not defile himself with the portion of the king's delicacies (Daniel 1:8).*

> *He encouraged them all that with purpose of heart they should continue with the Lord (Acts 11:23).*

The Bible heart "conceives" plans, "purposes" to act, "decides" on a course of action, "purposes in his heart" to carry out the plan. All of these are functions of the will of man—the Bible heart.

But the heart also includes man's intention: *"The thoughts and intents of the heart"* (Heb. 4:12). Because the heart includes the will of man, we are admonished,

> *Trust in the Lord with all your heart, and lean not on your own understanding (Prov. 3:5).*

Because the heart includes the will of man, we are commanded to believe. While many claim that they just cannot believe, the truth is that believing is an exercise of the will, and God commands it:

> *Believe on the Lord Jesus Christ, and you will be saved, you and your household (Acts: 16:31).*

Evidence Changes the Intellect

When Jacob saw the blood-smeared and torn coat, he "thought" his beloved Joseph was dead. The "evidence" led him to that conclusion. But, because he relied on the wrong evidence, his conclusion was wrong. We read of the miracles of Jesus,

> *And truly Jesus did many other signs in the presence of His disciples, which are not written in this book; but these are written that you may believe that Jesus is the Christ, the Son of God, and that, believing, you may have life in His name (John 20:30-31).*

The miracles of Jesus and the apostles, were to convince hearers that their message was from God. In other words, the miracles were evidence. And that evidence was to change their intellect, their thinking, and their convictions. That is what evidence does.

The Intellect Changes the Emotions

Far too many depend on their "feelings" to guide their thinking. They have put the cart before the horse! It is the thinking that produces the feelings. Look at Jacob and Joseph. When Jacob thought Joseph was dead, *"he mourned, and would not be comforted."* He felt sorrow for the death of his son—but his son was not dead. The way he felt was caused by what he thought. When he found Joseph was alive, he rejoiced. His feelings were real, both the sorrow and rejoicing. But the sorrow was based on the wrong intellectual conclusion.

The same principle is at work with us in the spiritual realm today. God loves us, and wants to save us from our sins (John 3:16). He sent His Son to die for us:

> *The goodness of God leads you to repentance (Rom. 2;4)*

> *Godly sorrow produces repentance leading to salvation (2 Cor. 7:10).*

God's goodness leads us to repentance by convincing us that we are sinners, producing sorrow for our sins, and recognizing that only Jesus can save us.

Intellect and Emotions Change the Will

When people are convinced that they are sinners, that only Jesus Christ can save them, their emotions are changed to produce love and gratitude. Their convictions and emotions then produce a change in the way they live. Look at the "prodigal son" in Luke 15. He left home, went to a far country and wasted his funds in sinful living. But in a hog pen he made a change. He saw where he was, he remembered home and his father, and the Scriptures say, *"He came to himself."* As a result, he determined (an exercise of his will) to go home. When he did, his father forgave him and restored him to his place in the family. Note that his intellect was changed first—he realized that the sinful lifestyle did not bring happiness. His emotions were then changed—he started thinking of home, and of going back. His will was then changed, and he determined to go back home.

That same pattern works in our spiritual lives today. Look at Acts 2. Peter preached Jesus as the Christ, the Savior. When people heard it, *"they were cut to the heart"* (v. 37) and asked what to do. God's answer, by Peter's mouth, was, *"Repent, and let every one of you be baptized in the name of Jesus Christ for the remission of sins"* (v. 38). Their response? *"Then those who gladly received his word were baptized"* (v. 41). Wasn't that simple? They changed their minds about their lifestyle, their godly sorrow led them to repentance and they were immediately baptized. Friend, the pattern has never changed. When people change their thinking about things by the evidence in the gospel, they are led to repentance, and that leads them to surrender their will to Christ to obey His commandments. They did it 2,000 years ago, and those who receive the word still do it!

Have you really given your heart to Jesus? Have you surrendered your convictions to His teachings, channeled your emotions to reciprocate His love, and then surrendered your will to Him by completely obeying Him? Note what the inspired apostle Paul wrote:

> *You obeyed from the heart that form of doctrine to which you were delivered. And having been set free from sin, you became slaves of righteousness (Rom 6:17-18).*

This morning I urge you to *"serve God with all your heart."* If there is anything we can do to help you with that, you may come forward and let us know, as we stand and sing.

CHRIST, OUR PASSOVER LAMB

Though the Old Testament abounds with a galaxy of prophecies, types, and figures which foreshadowed the coming of the Lord, none is more forceful nor more complete than that of the Paschal lamb and the Passover observance. This "type" in the period of Israel's deliverance portrays the future sacrificial offering of Jesus Christ in minute detail. And each part of the memorial observance of Israel's Passover shows us another facet of the event to be fulfilled in the greatest drama ever enacted before man.

The blood which flowed as an ever-widening stream from Israel's altars held no real meaning until the true Lamb of God shed His blood on the cross of Calvary. And the slaying of the Passover lamb was to have its true meaning revealed when the Christ should be offered for mankind. That you may get the full benefit from this study, I urge you, in your spare time, to turn back and study carefully the record in Ex. 12:1-46. You will then be able to clearly see the pattern of the type and anti-type perfectly revealed.

The Passover Lamb

The Paschal lamb was a fitting type of Jesus Christ. As a yearling of the sheep—being neither in infancy nor yet in old age—he represented the strength of the manhood in our Savior who died for us. The meekness and innocence of a lamb typified One who willingly submitted to the will of God. Hear the testimony of John:

The next day John saw Jesus coming toward him, and said, "Behold! The Lamb of God who takes away the sin of the world" (John 1:29).

Even in prophecy, the Messiah was pictured as a lamb being slain for His people,

He was oppressed and He was afflicted, yet He opened not His mouth; He was led as a lamb to the slaughter, and as a sheep before its shearers is silent, so He opened not His mouth (Isa. 53:7).

How fittingly our Lord was typified by the Passover lamb!

Chosen By The Father

The Paschal lamb was chosen by the father of the family (Ex. 12:3). In the same way, Christ was chosen of God, the Father of the spiritual house (John 3:16). Each house had its own Paschal lamb, for it could suffice for only one. Even so, the death of Christ was for only one house—the church of the Lord. Paul wrote of Jesus,

In Him we have redemption through His blood, the forgiveness of sins, according to the riches of His grace (Eph. 1:7).

There is only one house for which our Lord was slain, "

But if I am delayed, I write so that you may know how you ought to conduct yourself in the house of God, which is the church of the living God, the pillar and ground of the truth (1 Tim. 3:15).

Kept For Inspection

We are informed that the Paschal lamb was taken on the 10th day of the month of Abib (or Nisan, the first month of the year), and was then killed on the 14th day (Ex. 12:6). Thus it was kept for inspection for four days. It is, therefore, significant that Jesus Christ entered Jerusalem, in the sight of the multitude, on the day that the lamb was taken, and that He died on the day and the very hour that the paschal lamb was slain! The lamb had to be inspected to see that it was free from disease, and without blemish and spot. Jesus was taken (imprisoned), inspected (put on trial), and pronounced perfect by the ruler of the people, for Pilate declared,

> *Indeed, having examined Him in your presence, I have found no fault in this Man (Luke 23:14).*

Lamb without Blemish

The Paschal lamb had to be carefully inspected and found to be without any blemish (Ex. 12:5). Just as that Paschal lamb, Jesus was without defilement. Therefore, the apostle Peter could declare that we are redeemed

> *...with the precious blood of Christ, as of a lamb without blemish and without spot (1 Pet. 1:19).*

Truly, Jesus was one, *"Who committed no sin, nor was deceit found in His mouth"* (1 Pet. 2:22). Thus, the perfect Lamb of God was slain. And it is very interesting to note that He was placed on the cross at the time of the morning offering (the 3rd hour), and that He died at the time of the evening sacrifice (the 9th hour). Even as the Paschal lamb was roasted upon crossed sticks, so Jesus was placed upon a cross for us!

No Bones were Broken

The congregation joined in slaying the Paschal lamb, and the Jews and Gentiles joined in crucifying the Lord. A further type was shown in that God was careful to specify that no bones of the Passover lamb were to be broken (Ex. 12:46). But this was also true with the anti-type, our Passover, Jesus Christ:

> *He guards all his bones; Not one of them is broken (Psalm 34:20)*

> *Then the soldiers came and broke the legs of the first and of the other who was crucified with Him. But when they came to Jesus and saw that He was already dead, they did not break His legs ... For these things were done that the Scripture should be fulfilled, "Not one of His bones shall be broken" (John 19:32-36).*

The Blood Applied

One of the most arresting facets of this type is in the application of the blood. The blood of the Paschal lamb was sprinkled on the lintels and door-posts (Ex. 12:7). Those protected by that blood literally had to "pass through the blood" to enter the house of safety. In like manner, the blood of Jesus Christ was shed to purchase and protect His house, which is His church. The apostle Paul told the Ephesian elders:

Take heed to yourselves and to all the flock, among which the Holy Spirit has made you overseers, to shepherd the church of God which He purchased with His own blood (Acts 20:28).

The Israelites had safety only in the house protected by the blood of the Paschal lamb. In the same way, we have safety only in the house protected by the blood of Jesus Christ. There was no other place of refuge.

Redeemed By the Blood

Israel was redeemed from the death angel by the blood which was applied to their house. And Christians are redeemed only with the blood which purchased the house of the Lord. Paul wrote in Col. 1:14,

In whom we have redemption through his blood, the forgiveness of sins.

And the apostle Peter tells us that we are redeemed by this same blood (1 Pet. 1:18-19). As the apostle John wrote,

But if we walk in the light as He is in the light, we have fellowship with one another, and the blood of Jesus Christ His Son cleanses us from all sin (1 John 1:7).

The Supper Eaten

The eating of the Passover meal was enjoyed only by those who were protected and sheltered by the blood—that is, those in that house. Had it been otherwise, the Passover would have had no meaning at all. And the Lord's Supper is eaten only by these who have come into Christ, and have found refuge in His house, "which is the church" (1 Tim. 3:15). With Israel, the Passover supper was instituted in Egypt, but was observed principally after they had obtained their freedom from Egyptian bondage. The Lord's Supper was instituted "outside" the church (that is, before the church was established, Matt. 26:26-30). But His supper is to be eaten by those who are on the inside of His church. Israel ate the Passover meal with unleavened bread and bitter herbs (Num. 9:11). Christians eat the Lord's Supper with *"the unleavened bread of sincerity and truth"* in the midst of bitter trials (1 Cor. 5:7-8).

Passover Supper A Lasting Memorial

As Israel observed the Passover supper in memory of the passing over of the angel of death (Ex. 12:11-14), so Christians observe the Lord's Supper in memory of the One who died for us, in order that death would no longer hold power over us (Heb. 2:14-15). Just as Israel celebrated their deliverance, so Christians today celebrate the sacrifice that delivers us from the bondage of sin. And this, too, is to be a lasting memorial (Luke 22:19).

The Memorial Explained

When Israel observed the Passover, they were to fully explain the meaning of that supper from generation to generation (Deut. 16:3). Those who were not born into the family of Israel until after they departed from Egypt had to be told the importance of that supper. In the same fashion, Christians are to instruct one another, reminding each other of the meaning and the significance of the Supper which commemorates our deliverance:

> *For I received from the Lord that which I also delivered to you: that the Lord Jesus on the same night in which He was betrayed took bread; and when He had given thanks, He broke it and said, "Take, eat; this is My body which is broken for you; do this in remembrance of Me." In the same manner He also took the cup after supper, saying, "This cup is the new covenant in My blood. This do, as often as you drink it, in remembrance of Me." For as often as you eat this bread and drink this cup, you proclaim the Lord's death till He comes (1 Cor. 11:23-26).*

In closing, here are some very pertinent reminders. We should never overlook the place of blood in redemption. To find refuge, Israel had to be in the house sheltered by the blood. We, too, must be in the "house sheltered by the blood" of Jesus Christ. That means we must find and enter the church for which Jesus shed His blood. Moreover, we must pass through the blood in order to enter into this "*house of God, which is the church*" (1 Tim. 3:15). This we can do only if we are "*Baptized into Christ Jesus ... baptized into his death*" (Rom. 6:3-4). Study very carefully God's plan of Salvation. And if you have not already, enter into the true fold of safety by being baptized "*in the name of Jesus Christ for the remission of your sins*" (Acts 2:38) and by becoming a Christian, sheltered by the blood of our Paschal Lamb.

Achieving Unity in Religion

First of all, there can be no "Christian Unity" unless we believe, teach, and practice what Christ authorizes in the New Testament. Any system short of that would be mockery. It is one thing to agree upon the teachings of the Bible; it is quite another thing to just agree to disagree. The Lord commands to *"keep the unity of the Spirit in the bond of peace"* (Eph. 4:3). If the entire religious world were united on some doctrine that violated the Scriptures, it would not be the unity which Christ desires for us. There is a difference between union and unity. If we were to tie two cats together by their tails, and throw them over a clothes line, we would have union, but we certainly would not have unity!

Some Reasons for Religious Division

There is only one way to achieve unity in the Lord. It cannot be a matter of legislation by any hierarchy. Synods and councils cannot vote it into reality. In fact, such complex systems in religion help to create the "Babel" of voices already in our midst. The only answer is an open heart toward the word of God! Until men are willing to put aside denominational allegiance and sectarian strife, we will continue to see division running rampant. The creed books and catechisms, authored by men, have helped create the problem of division that exists. If we expect to achieve unity, we must leave all these behind and let Christ, the author of Christianity, rule our lives by the New Testament Scriptures.

In the United States, at the beginning of World War II, a fervent appeal was made to the entire nation. We were urged to be just Americans—not German-Americans, not Japanese-Americans, not Irish-Americans, not French-Americans—just Americans, nothing else. We need to drop the hyphenation in Christianity also! And for exactly the same reason—it divides people.

If we teach, practice, and obey the same message that was preached in the first century, we will be exactly what Paul, Peter, Philip, and Stephen were. They were Christians, members of the church which Jesus built. Nothing more, nothing less, nothing else! They were part of no denomination. We read all about the church they were members of in the New Testament. This is unity as Christ prayed for it in John 17:20-21. Nothing short of it will suffice. 1 Cor. 1:10 reads,

> *I plead with you, brethren, by the name of our Lord Jesus Christ, that you all speak the same thing, and that there be no divisions among you, but that you be perfectly joined together in the same mind and in the same judgment.*

Are we willing to pay the price to do just that? How glorious it is to be neither Catholic, Protestant, nor Jew—but just to be a Christian!

Is the Church of Christ a Denomination?

The church which Jesus established, according to the Scriptures, is the spiritual "body of Christ" over which our Lord rules as head (Col. 1:18, 24; Eph. 1:20-23). The church is not a building, nor a social club, nor a denomination, nor a political organization. The church which Jesus built (Matt. 16:18), and for which he died and shed His blood (Acts 20:28), is a divine institution authorized by God and promulgated by the gospel of His dear Son.

The church consists of those who have been added to it as a result of their obeying the simple commands of the head of the church, Jesus Christ. When people heard His gospel (Acts 2:16-26),

> *They were cut to the heart, and said to Peter and the rest of the apostles, Men and brethren, what shall we do? Then Peter said to them, Repent, and let every one of you be baptized in the name of Jesus Christ for the remission of your sins; and you shall receive the gift of the Holy Spirit ... Then those who gladly received his word were baptized; and that day about three thousand souls were added to them. ... And the Lord added to the church daily those who were being saved (Acts 2:37-38, 41, 47).*

Saved people are the church because the Lord who saves them puts them there.

Terms Applied in Scripture to the Church

The church of Christ is the kingdom of Christ. Our Redeemer rules over it as *"King of kings and Lord of lords."* Christians, members of that church, are citizens in the kingdom of heaven. And the gospel of Christ is the "seed of the kingdom" and the law of the kingdom.

The church of the Lord is His army, and members of the church are soldiers who *"put on the whole armor of God"* (Eph. 6:11). As the apostle Paul wrote,

> *Though we walk in the flesh, we do not war according to the flesh. For the weapons of our warfare are not carnal but mighty in God for pulling down strongholds, casting down arguments and every high thing that exalts itself against the knowledge of God, bringing every thought into captivity to the obedience of Christ (2 Cor. 10:3-4).*

So, the church is a militant force in the world, in a spiritual battle, not a carnal one.

The church is also the bride of Christ:

> *For the husband is head of the wife, as also Christ is head of the church; and He is the Savior of the body... Husbands, love your wives, just as Christ also loved the church and gave Himself for her... For this reason a man shall leave his father and mother and be joined to his wife... I speak concerning Christ and the church (Eph. 5:23-32).*

The church, therefore, should be pure and unblemished. To the church at Philippi, Paul said,

> *You may become blameless and harmless, children of God without fault in the midst of a crooked and perverse generation, among whom you shine as lights in the world (Phil. 2:15).*

What is the church? It is the "called out" group! The Greek word from which the term "church" is derived, literally means "the called out body." Paul writes that God has

> *...delivered us from the power of darkness and conveyed [translated, transferred] us into the kingdom of the Son of His love (Col. 1:13).*

The apostle Peter writes,

You also, as living stones, are being built up a spiritual house (1Pet. 2:5).

The church is composed of men and women who have been called out of sin, error and shame into the kingdom of Christ:

But you are a chosen generation, a royal priesthood, a holy nation, His own special people, that you may proclaim the praises of Him who called you out of darkness into His marvelous light (1 Pet. 2:9).

Certainly, from the above Scriptures, one can see how wonderful the church is in God's divine plan. You cannot afford to go through life without being a member of Christ's church. No, the church of the Lord, established in the first century, was not a denomination. The same church is not a denomination today. It has none of the characteristics of a sectarian body. According to the Scriptures, we read that the church is *"the fullness of Christ"* (Eph. 1:23)—not a segment, or part, of Him!

God Deplores Religious Division

The term, "denomination," means the number of times the unit is divided. Thus, when the bank teller asks, "What denominations do you want that $100 in?" and you reply, "Twenties," you have set the denomination of twenty for each bill. That is the way the $100 is divided. In the first century, after the beginning of the church in Jerusalem, division was condemned and never condoned. Read carefully 1 Cor. 1:10-13 where followers of Jesus were exhorted, *"Let there be no division among you"* and then asked, *"Is Christ divided?"* What if all religious people would honestly answer that question today?

And today we hear preachers and church leaders thank God for religious division! In every form of communication, we hear the plea, "Go to the church of your choice." This sincere, but mistaken, idea makes havoc of the prayer of our Lord in John 17:20-21, when He prayed that all those who believe might be one, even as He and the Father are. No, Christ did not shed His precious blood to purchase a denomination. The apostles did not set up sectarian groups as they preached the gospel. They simply established the church which Jesus had promised to build. That church has no earmarks of a denomination.

Jesus promised in Matt. 16:18, *"I will build my church."* We must go back to the Bible for that glorious body over which He rules as the head (Col. 1:18). May we all get back to the Bible! We must stop dividing the Church of the Lord.

Between the Sinner and Salvation

I am not responsible for the place baptism occupies in God's plan of salvation. Nor was I consulted in the matter. Had the Lord taken the matter up with me, maybe I would have very strongly advised against it. It has proved such a stumbling block to so many who are weak in faith. And, too, many have never had any faith in baptism for salvation! But I have a sublime faith in the One Who said, *"He that believes and is baptized shall be saved."* It is because of Him that I set forth His teaching on baptism.

Baptism seems to be a strange kind of command to so many people; maybe that is why the Lord set it in His plan of salvation. The idea of the ark probably didn't stack up as such a brilliant idea to those folk before it began to rain (Gen. 7)! And raising a brazen serpent wouldn't have been featured in many medical journals as a snake-bite remedy (Num. 21). And so far as research has determined, not many physicians advocated that lepers go and dip seven times in a muddy stream for cleansing (2 Kings 5). But God was not jesting when He declared,

> *"For My thoughts are not your thoughts, nor are your ways My ways," says the Lord. "For as the heavens are higher than the earth, so are My ways higher than your ways, and My thoughts than your thoughts" (Isa 55:8-9).*

No, maybe I wouldn't have put baptism into the saving plan, and maybe no other man would have. That, it seems to me, is evidence of God's work.

A Test of Faith

Baptism is a means by which God tests the faith of all who would serve Him. And if any man will not humbly obey the Lord in baptism, just as he obeys all other commands, then his faith is not what it ought to be. When the gospel was preached 2,000 years ago,

> *...Peter said to them, "Repent, and let every one of you be baptized in the name of Jesus Christ for the remission of sins" ... Then those who gladly received his word were baptized (Acts 2:38, 41).*

And when folk will not submit to this command (Acts 10:48), they thereby *"reject the will of God for themselves, not having been baptized"* (Luke 7:30).

Those who submit to baptism, as God has decreed, do not show faith in baptism—they show faith in the Lord who commands it!

> *Buried with Him in baptism, in which you also were raised with Him through faith in the working of God, who raised Him from the dead (Col 2:12).*

Therefore, obedience in being baptized shows faith in God—that, as He raised up Christ from the grave, He will also raise us up from the watery grave of baptism, in order that we may walk in *"newness of life"* (Rom. 6:3-4).

We Are Baptized Into Christ

God has placed baptism squarely between the alien sinner and every spiritual blessing. The Bible plainly says,

> *Blessed be the God and Father of our Lord Jesus Christ, who has blessed us with every spiritual blessing in the heavenly places in Christ (Eph. 1:3).*

And, notice the way we enter into Christ:

> *Or do you not know that as many of us as were baptized into Christ Jesus were baptized into His death? (Rom. 6:3)*

> *For you are all sons of God through faith in Christ Jesus. For as many of you as were baptized into Christ have put on Christ (Gal. 3:26-27).*

Because the only way the Bible reveals that we enter into Christ is by baptism, and every spiritual blessing is in Christ, it follows that we cannot reach a single spiritual blessing until we have been baptized into Christ. Man didn't arrange it that way; it is the work of the Lord. Man has no right to try any alterations. It is for man to accept God's plan, or reject the counsel of God which could save him.

Baptized ... Shall Be Saved

Let us notice the words of Jesus Christ in Mark 16:16.

> *He who believes and is baptized will be saved; but he who does not believe will be condemned (Mark 16:16).*

Here the Lord clearly placed baptism between the sinner and salvation. Notice in that Scripture that salvation follows baptism, that baptism is looking toward, or reaching toward, salvation. The words, "will be saved," plainly denote future action, not accomplished results. The sinner is baptized with hope in the promise that his sins shall be forgiven and he shall be saved from them!

Be Baptized ... Wash Away Your Sins

Saul, great persecutor of the Lord's church, had seen the Lord on the road to Damascus, and had asked the Lord what he was to do (Acts 22:10). After Saul had been praying for three days and nights, the Lord sent a man to him, and he was given to understand that he was not a saved man when Ananias came to him. The Lord's message was delivered by Ananias:

> *And now why are you waiting? Arise and be baptized, and wash away your sins, calling on the name of the Lord (Acts 22:16).*

Had his sins been forgiven, then this statement from a spokesman of the Lord would not have made sense. But Saul was still under the guilt of sin, and was to be pardoned only when he had been baptized into Christ.

For the Remission of Your Sins

An alien sinner reaches the remission of sins only through baptism. Baptism stands between him and this blessing.

> *Then Peter said to them, "Repent, and let every one of you be baptized in the name of Jesus Christ for the remission of sins" (Acts 2:38).*

To argue that remission of sins can be had before, or without, baptism is to go contrary to all the teaching of inspired men on the subject. Theologians and ecclesiasts may argue the matter from now until the dawn of eternity, but Acts 2:38 will still face them even then. It is not an option, but an imperative—it is a command to be obeyed. Sectarian delegates may get it removed from their church creed books, but it is still in God's Book!

Baptized Into His Death

Many religious folk emphasize how the blood of Christ cleanses us, and properly so. There is no remission without the blood of Jesus (Heb. 9:22; 10:4). But a lot of folks need to seriously consider that the only blood that can save is that which was shed in the DEATH of Christ. The apostle Paul wrote,

> *Or do you not know that as many of us as were baptized into Christ Jesus were baptized into His death? (Rom 6:3).*

There is no other means by which we can reach the blood of Jesus, save through His death, or in His body. His blood was shed in His death, and was then put into His spiritual body as its purchase price (Acts 20:28). Not only does Paul teach us that we are baptized into the death of Christ, but also he wrote:

> *For by one Spirit we were all baptized into one body—whether Jews or Greeks, whether slaves or free—and have all been made to drink into one Spirit (1 Cor. 12:13).*

Surely we must not minimize the blood of Christ as the cleansing power to wash away sins, but the blood is reached when we are baptized into His death, and thus come into His body, his church.

Baptized... Raised to Newness of Life

A new life is offered only after one has been baptized.

> *Or do you not know that as many of us as were baptized into Christ Jesus were baptized into His death? Therefore we were buried with Him through baptism into death, that just as Christ was raised from the dead by the glory of the Father, even so we also should walk in newness of life. For if we have been united together in the likeness of His death, certainly we also shall be in the likeness of His resurrection, knowing this, that our old man was crucified with Him, that the body of sin might be done away with, that we should no longer be slaves of sin (Rom 6:3-6).*

There must be the death, burial, and resurrection before this new life is possible. And that necessitates the act of baptism. We are baptized into Christ, and only then can we become new creatures:

Therefore, if anyone is in Christ, he is a new creation; old things have passed away; behold, all things have become new (2 Cor. 5:17).

Every statement on the subject places baptism between the sinner and the proposed spiritual blessing. This is a logical and expected arrangement when one realizes that all spiritual blessings are "in Christ" (Eph. 1:3), and that we are "baptized into Christ."

Baptized... Renewing of Holy Spirit

The apostle Paul wrote:

But when the kindness and the love of God our Savior toward man appeared, not by works of righteousness which we have done, but according to His mercy He saved us, through the washing of regeneration and renewing of the Holy Spirit (Titus 3:4-5).

There is no renewing of the Holy Spirit until there is the "washing of regeneration." This simply echoes what Peter preached on the day of Pentecost:

Then Peter said to them, "Repent, and let every one of you be baptized in the name of Jesus Christ for the remission of sins; and you shall receive the gift of the Holy Spirit" (Acts 2:38).

Only when one has been baptized is he given the Holy Spirit (1 Cor. 6:19-20), which is "*an earnest of our inheritance*" (Eph. 1:14).

Those who protest against baptism often use the argument that we are saved without works, and baptism is a work. But if we would please God, we must work the works of God (John 9:4). There is no question that baptism is the work of God, for He is the author of it. The truth is that we are saved by works of obedience, as the Bible plainly states (James 2:14-26). As Paul declared,

For in Christ Jesus neither circumcision nor uncircumcision avails anything, but faith working through love. (Gal. 5:6).

In all things, let us never forget that we reach and obtain every spiritual blessing in Christ, and that we are baptized into Jesus Christ.

A Spiritual Workout

One of the best things anyone can do for themselves is to exercise. Every doctor, every nutritionist and every "expert" on good physical health will tell you of your need for exercise. Sadly, in spite of the incredible amount of information available about working out, only a very small percentage of Americans actually participate in exercise. We all know it is good for us, but many fail to do it.

The same process is taking place in the spiritual realm as well. We live in a time where the Bible is readily available to all of us. Moreover, there are more Christian books, magazines, and online information available than ever in history. Yet, once again, many people are badly out of shape when it comes to their walk with God. How can we all get in better spiritual shape for the Lord?

Paul writes to Timothy and gives him advice on this subject.

> *For bodily exercise profits a little, but godliness is profitable for all things, having promise of the life that now is and of that which is to come. This is a faithful saying and worthy of all acceptance. For to this end we both labor and suffer reproach, because we trust in the living God, who is the Savior of all men, especially of those who believe. These things command and teach. Let no one despise your youth, but be an example to the believers in word, in conduct, in love, in spirit, in faith, in purity. Till I come, give attention to reading, to exhortation, to doctrine (1 Tim. 4:8-13).*

Paul writes these words at a later stage in the first century, when the church was functioning and active. Yet, it faced the same problems we do today. There were believers who were growing tired, who were not keeping up, who were losing their edge as they lived their daily lives. So Paul offers some spiritual exercises that would build up the preacher, Timothy. These exercises would then build up other believers as well.

You Must Be Active

One of the great principles of exercise is that you must do it yourself. You can read all about it, you can know all about it, but until you get up and do it, it will be of no benefit. All that knowledge is worthless if you are not getting up off the couch and doing something yourself.

Paul tells us that our faith is more than just what we know, it is what we do. He says we fix our hope (that is, our faith and confidence) on God, but he also says that we must labor and strive because of that hope. In other words, Paul says that knowing about God and His will motivates us to labor for God.

> *But be doers of the word, and not hearers only, deceiving yourselves (James 1:22).*

James echoes Paul's words by saying we are deceiving ourselves if we fail to be active in the service of God. Too many are content in their walk with God because they know all the right answers to all the questions and issues. Others are self-satisfied because they know the scriptures that prove this doctrinal point or that one. But knowing the word and not acting on the word is self-delusion. So James and Paul both say we must do more than merely *know* about the word, we must *apply* the word in our lives. James offers some ideas on this spiritual exercise.

> *If anyone among you thinks he is religious, and does not bridle his tongue but deceives his own heart, this one's religion is useless. Pure and undefiled religion before God and the Father is this: to visit orphans and widows in their trouble, and to keep oneself unspotted from the world (James 1:26-27).*

James says how we talk is a real test of our faith, not just what we know. James says how we respond to those less fortunate is a real measure of our spiritual health, not just how much we understand.

Paul adds some things in our first text. Paul mentions that faith, conduct, love, and purity are places every Christian can begin working out. When that takes place, our spiritual health will strengthen and we will know what is right, and we will do what is right.

You Must Trust the Word

Making the decision to exercise will make you healthier and happier. But it is a foolish person who just gets up one day and starts exerting themselves. All experts on exercise will tell you to consult a doctor before you start and will encourage you to use appropriate techniques as you try to improve your physical health. That means, if you are going to work out effectively, you must know what to do to get in shape. This was true for Timothy as well.

Paul tells Timothy to "*command and teach these things.*" Timothy was the preacher in this situation, but Paul knew that several things would happen when the word was taught. He knew Timothy would grow in the word himself. One of the great reasons for teaching others is that it forces the teacher to learn. In the process of building up the faith of others, the teacher always finds his/her faith built up as well.

> *But avoid foolish and ignorant disputes, knowing that they generate strife. And a servant of the Lord must not quarrel but be gentle to all, able to teach, patient, in humility correcting those who are in opposition, if God perhaps will grant them repentance, so that they may know the truth (2 Tim. 2:23-25).*

In his second letter Paul explains more about this process of building the teacher while building the hearers. Timothy was to avoid arguments, quarrels and such. These did not accomplish God's will, and instead would sidetrack Timothy from his real purpose, teaching and preaching the word. Further, Timothy would have to learn patience and gentleness, even with those who were in the opposition.

The purpose was to change others, but also to keep Timothy from straying as he tried to teach. If we are going to get in better spiritual condition, we must know what we are to do and believe and we should be active in sharing that with others. We also should avoid that which sidetracks our attention and draws us away from our work.

You Can Work Out With Others

One of the principles most fitness gurus talk about is a workout buddy. That is a person who walks or jogs with you. It is someone who will push you a little, motivate you to do a little more, someone you can encourage and who will encourage you. A workout buddy can make the process of getting in physical shape easier and more pleasant.

God tells us the same thing in terms of getting in better spiritual condition. Paul tells Timothy, "*…give attention to reading, to exhortation, to doctrine*." This is obviously referring to the public assemblies of the body of Christ. We are to assemble so we can get in better shape for the fight with Satan. The reason we assemble is not merely to worship God, although that will improve our spiritual condition. We do not come together just to say we made it to church. We assemble to improve our condition so we can better serve God in our daily lives.

> *And let us consider one another in order to stir up love and good works, not forsaking the assembling of ourselves together, as is the manner of some, but exhorting one another (Heb. 10:24-25a).*

Our goal when we assemble is to stimulate each other to more good works. Our times together help us encourage each other. If you want better spiritual health, start attending the worship services of the church on a regular basis.

This last point – on a regular basis—is critical. Too many ask "how many services must I attend to go to heaven?" This is like asking, "How little exercise can I get by with and still be in great shape?" The question is backwards. If you want to be in good physical shape, you will regularly run, jog, walk, or work out in some way. If you want to be in good spiritual condition you will attend the assemblies as much as you can. Instead of getting by with as little as possible, you will do as much as possible to achieve good spiritual health.

You Can Do It

There are many ways to get in shape physically. You can run or swim, you can jog or walk, you can lift weights or climb stairs. You have many options. There are many ways to get in spiritual shape as well. I have discussed only a few principles. You can pray more, you can study more, you can look for people to help, you can give more time or money to the Lord. All of these exercises will make your spiritual health stronger. But the bottom line is—YOU must do it.

No one can be saved for you and no one can keep you saved after you are in Christ. *You* had to believe. *You* had to repent. *You* had to be immersed. In the same way, *you* will have to study, to pray, to assemble and worship. No one can do this for you. Just as no one can *physically* work out for you, no one can *spiritually* work out for you either.

But, you can do it! The best news is that spiritual conditioning has even more resources and help than physical conditioning. God Himself will strengthen your faith when you get up and start working out spiritually. So, if you are on your spiritual couch, get off it! Learn what God wants and go at it. You can do it!

God – Who Is True

There are many characteristics of God.

God is love.

Beloved, let us love one another, for love is of God; and everyone who loves is born of God and knows God. He who does not love does not know God, for God is love. (1 John 4:7-8)

God is just.

For we must all appear before the judgment seat of Christ, that each one may receive the things done in the body, according to what he has done, whether good or bad. (2 Corinthians 5:10)

God can be severe.

Therefore consider the goodness and severity of God: on those who fell, severity; but toward you, goodness, if you continue in His goodness. Otherwise you also will be cut off. (Romans 11:22)

God is true. This last one is the characteristic we will focus on today.

It is the nature of God to be true.

That by two immutable things, in which it is impossible for God to lie, we might have strong consolation, who have fled for refuge to lay hold of the hope set before us (Hebrews 6:18).

He is the Rock, His work is perfect; for all His ways are justice, A God of truth and without injustice; righteous and upright is He (Deuteronomy 32:4).

Happy is he who has the God of Jacob for his help, whose hope is in the Lord his God, Who made heaven and earth, the sea, and all that is in them; Who keeps truth forever (Psalm 146:5-6).

He who blesses himself in the earth shall bless himself in the God of truth (Isaiah 65:16).

Indeed, let God be true but every man a liar. As it is written: "That You may be justified in Your words, and may overcome when You are judged" (Romans 3:4).

Seeing that it is the nature of God to be true, He has provided man with the proper means to know the truth – His word!

And now, O Lord God, You are God, and Your words are true, and You have promised this goodness to Your servant (2 Samuel 7:28).

All Scripture is given by inspiration of God, and is profitable for doctrine, for reproof, for correction, for instruction in righteousness, that the man of God may be complete, thoroughly equipped for every good work (2 Timothy 3:16-17).

Then Jesus said to those Jews who believed Him, "If you abide in My word, you are My disciples indeed. And you shall know the truth, and the truth shall make you free" (John 8:31-32).

Sanctify them by Your truth. Your word is truth (John 17:17).

Since God is true and His word is true, what does this mean to man?

The scriptures give man the opportunity to obtain knowledge. Christ said:

You search the Scriptures, for in them you think you have eternal life; and these are they which testify of Me (John 5:39).

Solomon wrote:

Happy is the man who finds wisdom, and the man who gains understanding (Proverbs 3:13).

Get wisdom! Get understanding! Do not forget, nor turn away from the words of my mouth (Proverbs 4:5).

Buy the truth, and do not sell it, also wisdom and instruction and understanding (Proverbs 23:23).

God has provided the means whereby we can know what is righteous and true, but knowledge is not going to be received through the process of osmosis. It will be our responsibility to study to obtain the knowledge.

The Scriptures give man direction.

David tells us:

Your word is a lamp to my feet and a light to my path (Psalm 119:105).

Man is lost and undone without the truth of God's word. The questions of life, "Why are we here?" and "After death, then what?" are all unanswerable without the Bible. It is the word of God that gives our lives meaning. It is the word of God that points us to our final reward. There is no way to determine right and wrong without the word of God. Man has tried and failed miserably! During the time of the judges we read:

In those days there was no king in Israel; everyone did what was right in his own eyes (Judges 21:25).

Do you know what that is called? Chaos or anarchy! There is no direction there.
Man has tried alternatives to what God is offering.

There is a way that seems right to a man, but its end is the way of death" (Prov. 14:12).

But the truth remains that Christ is the only way.

> *Jesus said to him, "I am the way, the truth, and the life. No one comes to the Father except through Me" (Jn. 14:6).*

> *"Nor is there salvation in any other, for there is no other name under heaven given among men by which we must be saved" (Acts 4:12).*

Without the truth of God's word, how would we know which way to go?

The Scriptures give man assurance. God is true. His word is true. Therefore, man can be assured of the promises and hope in Him.

Paul told Timothy:

> *You must continue in the things which you have learned and been assured of (2 Timothy 3:14).*

This is why Paul could say to Timothy:

> *...I know whom I have believed and am persuaded that He is able to keep what I have committed to Him until that Day (2 Tim. 1:12).*

I love that God is true because I can know where I stand with Him. So Can You.

Striving For the Faith of the Gospel

Only let your conduct be worthy of the gospel of Christ, so that whether I come and see you or am absent, I may hear of your affairs, that you stand fast in one spirit, with one mind striving together for the faith of the gospel (Phil. 1:27).

When the apostle Paul and his company of fellow-workers came to the city of Philippi, they found a remarkable city. Philippi was a "Roman City," built up to be a special garrison by the Romans to enhance the Roman Empire. The city, as a result, had a diverse population—Jews and Greeks, rich and poor, slave and free, people of various nationalities.

Paul had just left the province of Asia, in what is now Turkey, and entered for the first time into the continent of Europe. Philippi was his first stop in Europe. But the church which he planted here had a special place in Paul's heart.

I thank my God upon every remembrance of you, always in every prayer of mine making request for you all with joy, for your fellowship in the gospel from the first day until now (Phil. 1:3-5).

In this same letter, the apostle later told these Christians,

Therefore, my beloved, as you have always obeyed, not as in my presence only, but now much more in my absence, work out your own salvation with fear and trembling; for it is God who works in you both to will and to do for His good pleasure (Phil. 2:12-13).

In Phil. 1:27, Paul gives five things that make up the ingredients of a successful church of the Lord Jesus Christ. Let us look at them.

"Let Your Conduct Be Worthy"

The Lord Jesus constantly warns us to watch our speech and life. He warns us, *"Out of the abundance of the heart the mouth speaks"* (Matt. 12:34). Our speech reveals both who and what we are, and also whose we are! As Paul wrote,

Let no corrupt word proceed out of your mouth, but what is good for necessary edification, that it may impart grace to the hearers (Eph. 4:29).

The apostle Peter also warns of, *"laying aside all malice, all deceit, hypocrisy, envy, and all evil speaking"* (1 Pet. 2:1). Christians are to speak in such a way as to edify (build up) those who hear. Corrupt speech and evil speaking will not only corrupt us, it will degrade the church.

But our entire "manner of life [conduct]" must show that we belong to Christ. To become children of God we had to *"crucify the body of sin,"* be *"buried with Christ in baptism"* and then be *"raised to walk in newness of life"* (Rom. 6:3-6). Then let us live this new life as befits Him who died for us.

Do not lie to one another, since you have put off the old man with his deeds, and have put on the new man who is renewed in knowledge according to the image of Him who created him (Col. 3:9-10).

If we have been baptized "into Christ" (Rom. 6:3), then we are "new creatures in Christ" (2 Cor. 5:17), and we must live like it.

"That You Stand Fast"

To "stand fast" implies the determination to "*stand against the wiles of the devil*" (Eph. 6:11). As the apostle wrote,

That we should no longer be children, tossed to and fro and carried about with every wind of doctrine, by the trickery of men, in the cunning craftiness of deceitful plotting, but, speaking the truth in love, may grow up in all things into Him who is the head—Christ (Eph. 4:14-15).

Instead of acting with the capricious attitude of a child, we should be

...steadfast, immovable, always abounding in the work of the Lord (1 Cor. 15:58).

Stand fast.

Noah was given a big job: build a huge ark of about 500 feet in length, and preach to the folk of his generation about God's impending punishment (Gen. 6; 2 Pet. 2:5). But Noah, "by faith," stood fast and did his job.

Moses had the seemingly impossible job of leading a slave people out of Egypt and molding them into a great nation of people for God (Ex. 3 & 4). But Moses "stood fast" and did the job. The apostle Paul wrote:

As you therefore have received Christ Jesus the Lord, so walk in Him, rooted and built up in Him (Col. 2:6-7).

Watch, stand fast in the faith, be brave, be strong (1 Cor. 16:13).

To be a strong church, we must "stand fast."

"In One Spirit, With One Mind"

The Lord has always wanted His people to be united. Notice His prayer:

I do not pray for these [the apostles] alone, but also for those who will believe in Me through their word; that they all may be one, as You, Father, are in Me, and I in You; that they also may be one in Us, that the world may believe that You sent Me (John 17:20-21).

If we are to succeed as the Lord's people in His work, we must have the unity which He desires. Paul wrote,

Endeavoring to keep the unity of the Spirit in the bond of peace. There is one body and one Spirit, just as you were called in one hope of your calling; one Lord, one faith, one baptism; one God and Father of all (Eph. 4:3-6).

Look at the church in Jerusalem:

Then those who gladly received his word were baptized; and that day about three thousand souls were added to them. And they continued steadfastly in the apostles' doctrine and fellowship, in the breaking of bread, and in prayers ... Now all who believed were together ... So continuing daily with one accord in the temple, and breaking bread from house to house, they ate their food with gladness and simplicity of heart, praising God and having favor with all the people. And the Lord added to the church daily those who were being saved ... Now the multitude of those who believed were of one heart and one soul" (Acts 2:41-47; 4:32).

That is the kind of unity for which the Lord wants us all to strive.

Many people today will argue that all of the denominations that exist are good, and even are necessary, so that each can have "the church of his choice." But that idea is diametrically opposed to the prayer and the commandments of the Lord Jesus Christ! Notice what the word of God says about divisions in 1 Cor. 1:10-13.

Now I plead with you, brethren, by the name of our Lord Jesus Christ, that you all speak the same thing, and that there be no divisions among you, but that you be perfectly joined together in the same mind and in the same judgment. For it has been declared to me concerning you, my brethren, by those of Chloe's household, that there are contentions among you. Now I say this, that each of you says, "I am of Paul," or "I am of Apollos," or "I am of Cephas," or "I am of Christ." Is Christ divided? Was Paul crucified for you? Or were you baptized in the name of Paul?

The Lord wants all believers to be of "one spirit, one mind." To divide into denominations was wrong in Corinth 2000 years ago. It is still wrong today!

"Striving Together"

The word, "strive," means "fight, or contend." As Christians, we are in a battle—a spiritual battle.

For though we walk in the flesh, we do not war according to the flesh. For the weapons of our warfare are not carnal but mighty in God for pulling down strongholds, casting down arguments and every high thing that exalts itself against the knowledge of God, bringing every thought into captivity to the obedience of Christ (2 Cor. 10:3-5).

The apostle Paul exhorts us to wage the good warfare as we resist the devil. The armor of God is both our defense and our offense in this battle.

But the real emphasis in Paul's statement is found in the word "together." Our striving is much more effective as we work in fellowship with each other. The Bible speaks of our being united in effort as it describes the church as the "body of Christ" and each of us as members of His body (Rom. 12:4-5). Again,

> *For as the body is one and has many members, but all the members of that one body, being many, are one body, so also is Christ ... And if they were all one member, where would the body be? But now indeed there are many members, yet one body ... There should be no schism in the body, but that the members should have the same care for one another. And if one member suffers, all the members suffer with it; or if one member is honored, all the members rejoice with it. Now you are the body of Christ, and members individually (1 Cor. 12:12, 19-20, 25-27).*

Members of the body of Christ have different abilities which are used in different kinds of jobs, but all work together toward one goal in Christ.

"For the Faith of the Gospel"

We need always to remember to strive for the right thing. We must not contend for our own way or strive for our preferences. Instead, we are told, *"contend earnestly for the faith which was once for all delivered to the saints"* (Jude 3). We would like to think that everyone is honest and sincere, and that there are no false teachers in the world. But that just isn't true.

God gives us warning after warning:

> *Beloved, do not believe every spirit, but test the spirits, whether they are of God; because many false prophets have gone out into the world (1 John 4:1).*

> *Whoever transgresses and does not abide in the doctrine of Christ does not have God (2 John 9)*

> *But even if we, or an angel from heaven, preach any other gospel to you than what we have preached to you, let him be accursed (Gal. 1:8).*

Jesus told the apostles:

> *Go into all the world and preach the gospel to every creature. He who believes and is baptized will be saved (Mark 16:15-16).*

The apostle Paul said:

> *For I am not ashamed of the gospel of Christ, for it is the power of God to salvation (Rom. 1:16).*

That is what we must "strive together" for—the gospel of Christ. Early Christians certainly knew that. When persecution came, and the disciples had to flee the city of Jerusalem, *"those who were scattered went everywhere preaching the word"* (Acts 8:4). The Christians of whom we read in the Bible heard the gospel, they believed the gospel, they obeyed the gospel, they lived the gospel, and they preached the gospel.

If we would be the church which Christ wants us to be, we must heed the admonition as the church at Philippi did:

> *Only let your conduct be worthy of the gospel of Christ, so that whether I come and see you or am absent, I may hear of your affairs, that you stand fast in one spirit, with one mind striving together for the faith of the gospel (Phil. 1:27).*

Sin: From All Sides

A preacher was preaching on brotherly love. He asked his audience if anyone could honestly say he didn't have a single enemy. Well this one old guy stood up and said "I don't!" The preacher commended the old man and asked him to share his secret with the church. "Tell us how you managed to be without enemies." The old man spoke up and said, "I outlived every one of those skunks."

This silly story demonstrates how we often attempt to obey God. We want to be right with God, but we want to do it our way. Now, Jesus constantly confronted this sort of issue in the people of His time. In Luke 7 we read of an event that shows how people struggled to be right with God when they encountered Jesus. In this encounter we meet two different kinds of sinners. And in this story we see the attitude of God toward sinners of all kinds.

So let's go to the scene. Turn to Luke 7 and let's read verses 36-50…

> *Then one of the Pharisees asked Him to eat with him. And He went to the Pharisee's house, and sat down to eat. And behold, a woman in the city who was a sinner, when she knew that Jesus sat at the table in the Pharisee's house, brought an alabaster flask of fragrant oil, and stood at His feet behind Him weeping; and she began to wash His feet with her tears, and wiped them with the hair of her head; and she kissed His feet and anointed them with the fragrant oil. Now when the Pharisee who had invited Him saw this, he spoke to himself, saying, "This Man, if He were a prophet, would know who and what manner of woman this is who is touching Him, for she is a sinner."*
>
> *And Jesus answered and said to him, "Simon, I have something to say to you." So he said, "Teacher, say it." "There was a certain creditor who had two debtors. One owed five hundred denarii, and the other fifty. And when they had nothing with which to repay, he freely forgave them both. Tell Me, therefore, which of them will love him more?"*
>
> *Simon answered and said, "I suppose the one whom he forgave more." And He said to him, "You have rightly judged." Then He turned to the woman and said to Simon, "Do you see this woman? I entered your house; you gave Me no water for My feet, but she has washed My feet with her tears and wiped them with the hair of her head. You gave Me no kiss, but this woman has not ceased to kiss My feet since the time I came in. You did not anoint My head with oil, but this woman has anointed My feet with fragrant oil. Therefore I say to you, her sins, which are many, are forgiven, for she loved much. But to whom little is forgiven, the same loves little."*
>
> *Then He said to her, "Your sins are forgiven." And those who sat at the table with Him began to say to themselves, "Who is this who even forgives sins?" Then He said to the woman, "Your faith has saved you. Go in peace."*

A Sinner Who Knows It

The woman in this text was well known as a sinner. No one, including Jesus, disputes the fact that she deserves her reputation. Some think she may have been a prostitute, others believe that she was a "fallen woman" with many lovers. Some think that she may have been a thief or con artist of some sort. The truth is, we are not told what her sin was; but whatever her sin, she made no pretense about being a good person. She made no defense; she did not even try to pretend that she was not what everyone thought she was.

The woman came to Jesus offering an expensive gift. This gift symbolized two important aspects of the culture. The anointing of perfume was done to kings, to positions of importance. Without realizing it, this sinful woman was proclaiming Jesus to be a king. But anointing was also done to corpses, to prepare them for burial. Again, without realizing it, the woman was pointing ahead to the time Jesus would die for all sinners, including her. Her actions declared Jesus to be both king and savior.

This woman knew she was a sinner, but out of her love for Jesus she approached Him. This should encourage ANYONE who is caught up in ANY sin. There is never a time or a place that Jesus will not accept a sinner who comes to Him in faith and love. Jesus will even accept a notorious sinner—one the whole community has decided is unworthy… Kind of like this woman.

Some will object to this, just as the critics in this story objected. How can we live sinful lives, then throw ourselves on God and expect Him to forgive us? But, that is the whole point of this story. Jesus (God) loves all people and will receive any sinner who comes in love and faith. Even though a sinner can never make up for his or her sins, Jesus will lovingly and willingly take any sinner who knows it and will come to Him.

A Sinner Who Doesn't Know It

Simon was a Pharisee. They were careful and strict in obeying each and every one of God's laws. They prided themselves on their performance of the Law of Moses. But, the Pharisees as a group (and Simon as an individual) had not made up their minds about Jesus. So, Simon was interested in Jesus, even inviting Him to dinner. He wanted to understand Jesus better, but not by fully accepting Him. Simon failed to do the socially accepted things. He offered Jesus no water for His feet, which was expected in social circles. Simon would not kiss Jesus, the equivalent of a hand shake today. In other words, Simon was not even offering Jesus the normal courteous actions of His day. So you see, the Pharisee seemed willing to eat with Jesus, but not fully accept Him.

Simon is like many sinners today. They don't even realize they are sinners. He was so full of his own righteousness that he could not commit to the One who was righteous. Simon was sitting with the Son of God, but couldn't see it since he was blinded by his own prejudice and pride. Many sinners today are like that as well. They think they are "good people" and that they will be alright with God since they are good. But, blinded by their pride, they miss the Son of God and His invitation to all sinners to be saved.

Jesus tried to get Simon to see this. He told him about the man who was owed by two different debtors. Simon could see the point, but apparently could not apply it to himself. Both sinners in Jesus' parable owed a debt, one was huge, the other much smaller. But still, both were in debt and unable to pay. The woman was a sinner with an enormous debt, but could not pay it. However, Simon was also a sinner with a debt he could not pay.

But Simon would not or could not see his position. All he could see was that Jesus was comfortable with sinners. What Simon failed to grasp was this: if sinners cannot approach Jesus, if sinners cannot approach God, then even Simon could not come to God! Jesus tells this parable to open Simon's eyes; but the critics seem to fail to get the message that God will accept and welcome all sinners. People may be surprised at this, but the message of Luke 7 is clear: Jesus (God) will forgive and save anyone.

A Savior Who Loves All Sinners

The most remarkable part of this story is Jesus. He is a Lord who loves all kinds of sinners. He certainly accepts the notorious woman. She brazenly enters a Pharisee's house (an unheard of thing) and touches a man, which women were not supposed to do. Her gift was expensive, but she was clearly a known sinner and was also behaving in a very scandalous way for her time. But still, Jesus loved her and accepted her gift. He even forgave her of whatever sins she may have committed. The people around the Lord were amazed and perhaps shocked, but He loved all sinners, even the notorious ones.

Jesus had already proven His love for sinners in even showing up at this dinner. Although Simon was unwilling to be courteous and kind while he "inspected" Jesus, the Lord went to the dinner and ate and talked with the other sinners in the story. Jesus knew Simon was wrong in his heart and in his attitude. But, Jesus loves all sinners, even those who are so full of pride they don't know they are sinners. The Lord attended this gathering, was treated rudely, but still He went because He cared about Simon. Jesus loves all sinners no matter what their sin. So, the Lord accepted Simon's invitation and the woman's appreciation.

A Savior Who Accepts All Sinners

Jesus still accepts all kinds of sinners. The good news about the Lord is that no matter what you have done (or left undone) you are loved by God. Jesus will take you back, if your gift is expensive or cheap, if your sin is huge or small. Jesus will accept you if you will come to Him. Some think their crimes are too severe, that God would never accept them back. But God will.

Sadly, many are like Simon, sure they are good but the people around them are evil. So, some sit in judgment of sinners, labeling them as notorious and unworthy. These proud people would never think it all right for a sinner to get close to God. But Jesus still accepts those sinners. You bring your gift to God and Jesus will accept you, regardless of your past or your failings or the size of your gift. This may offend some who are proud, but the Lord will take you back.

Still, there are many sinners who are unaware they are sinners. We must learn to love them just as Jesus did. This is not always easy, as pride and arrogance are offensive to most of us. But Jesus looked beyond the personal insults Simon offered Him. Instead, Jesus saw another sinner in need of a Savior. Jesus reached out, patiently and kindly, even to the proud sinner. This too must be our task, to love the notorious sinners as Jesus did, and to treat the proud sinners as Jesus did.

Accept This Savior

We have seen sin from all sides in this event. We have seen two sinners, with different backgrounds and attitudes, but both in need of forgiveness. Jesus loves them both and treats each with dignity and compassion. That is the Savior that awaits your return. The fact is, *"all have sinned and fall short of the glory of God"* (Rom. 3:23). All of us are sinners. Some of us, like this woman, know we are sinners and unworthy of God's love and grace. Others are proud, unwilling to admit they are sinners. But still, all have sinned. Jesus both loves and died for you, whether you know it and appreciate it or not.

Don't let pride get in the way of your salvation. Jesus will forgive any who come to the cross and are forgiven by His blood. Look with me at Gal. 3:26-27.

If you, a sinner, come to the Lord in faith and clothe yourself with Him in baptism, you can be saved today. Don't be proud and think you don't need a Savior. Don't be proud and think you don't need to believe or be baptized. Just come to Him, accept Him, and He will accept you.

Let us stand and sing.

An Unlikely Place

There are so many things I enjoy about the Christmas holidays. There is time for family, for being with friends and loved ones. There is, it seems to me, more caring, more compassion and good-will among people. The holiday season can certainly be refreshing.

But a great deal about Christmas is shrouded in myth and tradition. The Bible gives no date for the birth of Jesus. History tells us that the early church did not celebrate the birth of Jesus at all for over three hundred years. The first observances of the birth of Jesus started in the fourth century to lure people away from the worship of the pagan God, Mithra. The December date was chosen to coincide with a festival held in that false god's honor each winter. In different lands and cultures, different dates for the birth of Jesus are honored. Puritan England and the colonists of New England banned the celebration of Christmas altogether. On we could go, examining the myths and traditions that surround the birth of Jesus.

It is smart to be careful about separating myth from fact, especially in the realm of faith and salvation. It is smart to dismiss human traditions, especially those that elevate things that God has not stressed. But, in dismissing the myths that surround the birth of Jesus, don't dismiss the event itself. And we shouldn't dismiss the ***fact*** that at this time of year, perhaps more than any other time of year, people are thinking about the Savior. In the birth of Jesus, God reveals Himself to man as never before. And in the birth of Jesus, we learn much about God and His will and His ways. As with much that God does, the birth of Jesus occurs in the most unlikely place.

> *And it came to pass in those days that a decree went out from Caesar Augustus that all the world should be registered. This census first took place while Quirinius was governing Syria. So all went to be registered, everyone to his own city.*
>
> *Joseph also went up from Galilee, out of the city of Nazareth, into Judea, to the city of David, which is called Bethlehem, because he was of the house and lineage of David, to be registered with Mary, his betrothed wife, who was with child. So it was, that while they were there, the days were completed for her to be delivered. And she brought forth her firstborn Son, and wrapped Him in swaddling cloths, and laid Him in a manger, because there was no room for them in the inn (Luke 2:1-7).*

The Town of Bethlehem

Jesus was born in a little village a few miles from Jerusalem. Bethlehem had little claim to fame. It was the home town of David, Israel's greatest and most revered king. Because Joseph and Mary were of the lineage of David, they had to go to this town for the census. Bethlehem's other reason for importance was the prophecy of Micah.

> *But you, Bethlehem Ephrathah, though you are little among the thousands of Judah, yet out of you shall come forth to Me the One to be Ruler in Israel, whose goings forth are from of old, from everlasting (Micah 5:2).*

When the magi (or, "wise men") from the East arrived some time later, the Jewish scholars in Jerusalem knew to send them to Bethlehem to find the new born king of the Jews (Matt. 2:1-15). But, other than that, this little village had no importance at all. It was probably pastoral in character, some farming and herding making up the main occupation.

From Heaven to Bethlehem

The amazing thing is that God sent Jesus to start His life and work in a place like this. Jesus had spent eternity in God's presence.

> *In the beginning was the Word, and the Word was with God, and the Word was God. He was in the beginning with God (John 1:1-2).*

Jesus was God and was with God before that little city called Bethlehem ever existed. Yet, when it was time for Jesus to be born and live on earth, God chose this place for it all to begin.

The night He was born was nothing special to anyone, except Joseph and Mary. The town was busy, probably full of people for the census. The Romans were busy, taking everyone's name and getting facts straight for the process of taxing their subjects. All around, life was moving along at normal, hectic speed. Meanwhile, God comes to earth as a baby, born to redeem all mankind. But most people that night completely missed it.

In this aspect, Bethlehem was like our world today. People are busy. Some are hard at work making a living. Others are full of duties and obligations to family or organizations. Much of the busy-ness is not evil in and of itself. But in the busy-ness we too often miss the importance of the Son of God.

Like the people on the night Jesus was born, we can get so caught up in life's duties and needs, that we forget that God became flesh and lived among us.

> *And the Word became flesh, and dwelt among us, and we beheld His glory, glory as of the only begotten from the Father, full of grace and truth (John 1:14).*

The significance of the arrival of the Son of God can be obscured to us because of our hectic lifestyles. But the fact is important to your eternal future. Jesus became flesh to show us the Father's glory, His grace and truth. Don't let life's busy-ness keep you from seeking the Son of God who came to save you.

The Manger

For whatever reasons, there was no room in the inn. Perhaps the inn was full to overflowing due to the census, so that there were no rooms available. Perhaps Joseph and Mary were too poor to afford the room, so there was no room for them. We don't know the details, we just know the Son of God, who came to redeem man, was born and laid in a manger. We may not know all the details of why they found themselves in this situation, but one thing we do know, this is not the place for a king to be born, let alone a place for the King of kings to be born!

It was in these humble circumstances that Jesus breathed His first earthly breath. It was surrounded by animals, straw, and two loving parents that Jesus found Himself on earth. What a scene, the Son of the Almighty God, starting life in a feeding trough!

From Angels to a Feeding Trough

From eternity Jesus had been in heaven with God. He had been surrounded by the same heavenly host that accompanies God at all times. The same angels that would praise God later that same night (Luke 2:8ff) had been with Jesus in heaven. Now, this same divine being finds Himself surrounded, not by the heavenly host He deserves, but by the sights, sounds, and smells of a manger and its surroundings.

Jesus was not born into luxury. When He arrived on earth it wasn't in a five-star hotel with 24-hour room service. There were no satin sheets and maids to tend to Him. His life did not begin with the honor He deserved. Jesus did not begin life with a silver spoon in His mouth and all the advantages a wealthy family could provide. He did not start out in the center of earth's power, in a royal family at the center of political power. He was born to parents of lowly circumstance.

Jesus accepted this humble position for one reason. He wanted you to be with Him. He knew that we could never be in heaven with Him, since we were sinners.

For all have sinned and fall short of the glory of God (Rom. 3:23).

But Jesus did not want to leave you in your sin. Knowing that we could not join Him in heaven due to our sin, He left heaven to live among us, even with our sin. Jesus accepted the humility of a manger, and the humility of being human at all, so that we could be forgiven, and one day, join Him in heaven. God knew the only way to do that was for Jesus to come to us; since we could never get to Him on our own.

When Jesus was born, the young couple had no baby bed for Him. They used the most convenient thing they could find, they used the feeding trough. A manger would be just the right shape and size to hold a newborn baby. And his "baby clothes" were "swaddling clothes." It was in the most humble of settings that God became flesh.

From a Throne to a Baby

Jesus deserved a throne. He had been with God from the beginning and deserved the highest place and highest praise man could offer. This baby, of all babies ever born, deserved the best that man could give. Yet, He left His deserved place of honor and accepted the lowest place of humanity.

The most remarkable aspect to the birth of Jesus, for many, is that God was wrapped up in the form of a baby. A human baby is the most helpless of creatures, totally dependent on its mother. Jesus took this fragile place, risking all that life could throw at Him. God comes to earth, not as a powerful ruler or conquering king, but as a newborn baby boy.

Jesus did this so that you and I would know that He understands us and our needs. If Jesus had been born into luxury and power, into privilege and status, who among us would think He could understand our lives? But Jesus understands all you experience, because He went through it, too. If Jesus had come as the powerful being He truly is, who would think He could understand our sin, our weaknesses, our hurts? But He came as a baby, lived life for 33 years just as you and I live it. He did this so you and I could know that He gets it, He understands our hurts and our struggles.

For we do not have a high priest who cannot sympathize with our weaknesses, but One who has been tempted in all things as we are, yet without sin. Let us therefore draw near with confidence to the throne of grace, that we may receive mercy and may find grace to help in time of need (Heb. 4:15-16).

Jesus could not have done that if He had come in the glory and honor He deserved. So, He accepted the most dependent status on earth, the form of a newborn baby.

Your Heart

Perhaps there is one other unlikely place for Jesus to be born, and that is within you. It is most challenging to realize that Jesus was born in the unlikely city of Bethlehem, laid in a manger as a baby, all to give you the chance to be right with God. No matter what your sin is, no matter what you have done, no matter how unlikely it seems that God can live in you—still, Jesus wants you to be born again (John 3:3-5), so He can lay claim to your heart.

As you look at your life, you may not think there is room for the Son of God. But if you will put your faith in Him, leave your sin and be immersed in His name (Acts 2:38; Rom. 6:3-4), you too, can experience a birth, a new birth of water and the Spirit. And in the most unlikely place of all—your heart—God will live. Accept Jesus and His gift of salvation today.

No Man Asked: "What Have I Done?"

The prophet of old, looking at the rebellion and the indifference of God's people, wrote:

Thus says the Lord ... "I listened and heard, but they do not speak aright. No man repented of his wickedness, saying, 'What have I done?' Everyone turned to his own course, as the horse rushes into the battle" (Jer. 8:4-6).

This is the time of year when businessmen take inventory, checking their books and their goods to find out what they have done during the year. As a result, they can better plan the new year. But, in the spiritual realm, shouldn't we also take inventory? As we look back over the past year, shouldn't we also ask the question of ourselves, "What have I done?"

What Have I Done for the Lord?

As we conclude the year, can we honestly say that we have improved in our service to the Lord Jesus Christ? There are ways to get the answer to that. When Jesus pictured the scene of the judgment, as recorded in Matt. 25, He said,

Then the King will say to those on His right hand, "Come, you blessed of My Father, inherit the kingdom prepared for you from the foundation of the world: for I was hungry and you gave Me food; I was thirsty and you gave Me drink; I was a stranger and you took Me in; I was naked and you clothed Me; I was sick and you visited Me; I was in prison and you came to Me." Then the righteous will answer Him, saying, "Lord, when did we see You hungry and feed You, or thirsty and give You drink? When did we see You a stranger and take You in, or naked and clothe You? Or when did we see You sick, or in prison, and come to You?" And the King will answer and say to them, "Assuredly, I say to you, inasmuch as you did it to one of the least of these My brethren, you did it to Me."

Then He will also say to those on the left hand, "Depart from Me, you cursed, into the everlasting fire prepared for the devil and his angels: for I was hungry and you gave Me no food; I was thirsty and you gave Me no drink; I was a stranger and you did not take Me in, naked and you did not clothe Me, sick and in prison and you did not visit Me." Then they also will answer Him, saying, "Lord, when did we see You hungry or thirsty or a stranger or naked or sick or in prison, and did not minister to You?" Then He will answer them, saying, "Assuredly, I say to you, inasmuch as you did not do it to one of the least of these, you did not do it to Me." And these will go away into everlasting punishment, but the righteous into eternal life. (Matt. 25:34-46).

I can easily test "what have I done" for the Lord by looking at what I have done for other people. You can easily test yourself as well by the same standard. In our world there are the depressed, the lonely, the sad, the troubled, the bereaved, the sick, the abused, the hopeless, the neglected. Should we not look at those people, and then ask ourselves, "What have I done" for those folks? How I can claim to be a follower of Jesus, if I look the other way while these people are suffering? The Lord "*went about doing good*" (Acts 10:38). This means, if we are going to strive to be like Him, we must do good also.

What Have I Done for My Spiritual Growth?

Are we at the same level of spirituality as last year at this time? If so, shame on us! The Lord expects us to grow.

> *You therefore, my son, be strong in the grace that is in Christ Jesus (2 Tim. 2:1).*

> *But grow in the grace and knowledge of our Lord and Savior Jesus Christ (2 Peter 3:18).*

> *We should no longer be children, tossed to and fro and carried about with every wind of doctrine, by the trickery of men, in the cunning craftiness of deceitful plotting, but, speaking the truth in love, may grow up in all things into Him who is the head—Christ (Eph. 4:14-15).*

Have I done that in the past year? Have you?

The apostle Paul says:

> *Examine yourselves as to whether you are in the faith. Test yourselves (2 Cor. 13:5).*

As in the physical realm, so in the spiritual, there are two things vital to growth: food and exercise. The apostle Peter writes:

> *As newborn babes, desire the pure milk of the word, that you may grow thereby (1 Pet. 2:2).*

And the apostle Paul exhorts us,

> *Exercise yourself toward godliness (1 Tim. 4:7-8).*

If we absorb of the word of God, and live by it, we will grow in Christ.

What Have I Done for the Church?

Jesus promised, "*I will build my church*" (Matt. 16:18). The apostle Paul declared that He "*purchased the church with his own blood*" (Acts 20:28). The Lord adds the saved to that church (Acts 2:47). Shouldn't that church be important enough, then, to have priority in our lives throughout the year? Jesus said it:

> *Seek first the kingdom of God and His righteousness (Matt. 6:33).*

As members of the church of Christ, what have I done? What have you done? Let us look back over our lives in this year and "test ourselves." Have I attended all of the services of the church, "*not forsaking the assembling of ourselves together, as is the manner of some, but exhorting one another*" (Hebrews 10:25)? Have I encouraged the leadership and prayed for them? Have I given liberally of my income to fund the work of the church? Have I constantly "talked up" the church of which I am a member and which affords me so many spiritual blessings? Or are my words full of negativity?

What Have I Done for the Lost?

Jesus Christ *"came into the world to save sinners"* (1 Tim. 1:15). Because He came to *"seek and to save the lost"* (Luke 19:10), so must I. I hear His words, *"Go into all the world and preach the gospel to every creature"* (Mark 16:15). Paul says we should not be ashamed of the gospel for it is *"the power of God to salvation"* (Rom. 1:16). You know, I have come into contact with members of the Lord's church who were afraid to tell me that they were members of the church of Christ. I have spoken with folks who were nervous about revealing to me that they read the Bible, as if they were ashamed of the word of God. We should not be ashamed of the Lord's church. We should not be ashamed of the Gospel, for in it the righteousness of God is revealed from faith to faith.

Being unashamed of the gospel, we must share it. If the lost do not hear, how shall they believe and be saved? And if I, a Christian, do not tell the story of Jesus, who will? As the apostle Paul wrote, *"We believe, and therefore we speak"* (2 Cor. 4:13). The cry of the inspired psalmist should ring in our ears: *"Let the redeemed of the Lord say so!"* (Psa. 107:2). We need to do more in the next year! How many "lepers" have we reached out to in compassion and touched? We must not be like the Pharisee who prayed, "thank God I'm not like those sinners." That is not pleasing to God. He wants us to touch that sinner. He wants His word to have the ability to prick the heart of that sinner. And that will only be possible through the compassion of us who have been saved from our own diseases. Have you reached out to the lost? If not, purpose in your heart to do better. Don't just make it a resolution, make it a lifestyle!

Many times we think, "What can I do better in the coming year so that I will be more acceptable to God?" Well, the truth is, before you can look forward at what you can do or will do, you must take a survey of what you have done. Without that, there is no standard. We see that clearly in Scripture. So if you have failed in any of these categories, determine your shortcomings, and insist on improvements in those areas. You only have control of one soul on this earth—yours. If your soul is lost to spend an eternity in hell, it will be because you didn't repent, saying "what have I done?"

About the Author

Mitch Robison is a Gospel minister, a missionary, a husband, a father, and a servant. A native of Georgia, he currently serves as the pulpit minister for the Pleasant Grove Rd. Church of Christ in Inverness, FL.

Mitch began his studies at the Georgia School of Preaching in 2008. In 2009, he began to serve the Cedar Grove Church of Christ in Fairburn, GA as their associate minister. He is grateful for the great Christians there who taught him so much about being a genuine man of God.

In 2015 Mitch began work as a full-time minister for the Enon Church of Christ in Webb, AL. He served there for 2 ½ years, continuing to grow in knowledge of the Scripture. The time at Enon allowed him to begin emphasizing his mission mindedness. He organized several mission efforts locally and within the southeast region.

In 2018 Mitch began to serve the Christians of the Pleasant Grove Rd. church in Inverness, FL. This opportunity has allowed him to have continued growth in many aspects of his Christian walk, including his focus on authentic Christianity and missions, both in the community and the region.

In 2004 Mitch married his beautiful wife Katy. She has served by his side as an encourager, teacher, and example of an authentic Christian woman. In 2008, they were blessed with their daughter Sadie (Mitch had been hoping to have a little girl). In 2011, their son Eli was born. Mitch takes a lot of pride in Eli and strives daily to be a positive example of a Christian man to his son.

If you have a desire to contact Mitch, feel free to do so!

Phone – 678-953-1510
Email – mitchpgr@gmail.com
Mail – 5641 S. Burr Terrace,
Inverness, FL 34452

www.ingramcontent.com/pod-product-compliance
Lightning Source LLC
Chambersburg PA
CBHW081355040426
42451CB00017B/3453